Archaeology
of the
Jordan Valley

Elmer B. Smick

2743

BAKER BOOK HOUSE ● Grand Rapids, Michigan

Dedicated
to Jane

PICTURE CREDITS:

Israel Government Tourist Office, 12, 18, 22
Matson Photo Service, 20, 37, 49, 62, 72, 114 (bottom), 118, 120, 130,
  134, 136
Levant Photo Service, 110, 112, 130
Israel Office of Information, 68, 117 (middle), 126
Philadelphia University Museum, 77, 79, 84, 88, 89
Elmer B. Smick, 14, 17, 38, 42, 43, 46, 73, 75, 82, 86, 114 (top), 117
  (top and bottom), 123
Israel Office of Information, 68, 117 (middle), 126

The sketches of the Madaba Map were based on Michael Avi-Yonah's
maps in *The Madaba Mosaic Map with Introduction and Commentary*
published by the Israel Exploration Society. Other maps sketches were
drawn by the author using a variety of sources as references.

Copyright © 1973
by Baker Book House Company
ISBN: 0-8010-7951-9
Printed in the United States of America

PREFACE

The writing of this volume is a result of a paper, "The Jordan of Jericho," delivered at the Evangelical Theological Society. The paper was an attempt to deal with the apparent problem in those verses of the Old Testament which describe all the territory east of the Jordan River (Reuben, Gad, and half tribe of Manasseh) as *Yardēn Yerēḥō*, which was usually translated "the Jordan opposite Jericho"—which of course does not make sense for such an extended area. The "error" has been attributed to an author or scribe who was not thinking when he wrote. However, the phrase is used often enough to make one suspicious of this explanation. In the paper I discussed this explanation along with Professor Cyrus Gordon's contention that the word *Yarden* was really an East Mediterranean word meaning "river." The discussion in a more popular form is summarized in chapter two.

The rest of this book is an attempt to familiarize the average Biblically oriented reader with the progress made by the modern archaeological movement in the Jordan Valley. Residence in Israel and Jordan before and after the Six Day War has given me a firsthand knowledge of the valley, its geography and archaeology, but I make no attempt to identify myself as a seasoned field archaeologist. The archaeological work of the late Professor Nelson Glueck and his lucid writing on this area are much appreciated. I hope that an occasional difference with his views will not be considered presumptuous.

In this book I follow the Biblical references to the Jordan Valley, departing where deemed necessary to fill out the picture, as, for example, in surveying the prehistoric and Early Bronze periods and occasionally touching on non-Biblical Jewish history.

The archaeology of the Jordan Valley partially represents the archaeology of Palestine, just as the latter is partially representative of the archaeology of the Near East, which in turn is only a part of a wider scope which includes all western Asia and the Mediterranean countries. Any apology for considering only a segment of Palestine is equally valid for considering only Palestine, or for that matter considering only a single location. Each segment must be viewed in its wider context. I have tried to use this as a principle in dealing with the Jordan Valley.

By concentrating on a limited area I have attempted to give the reader and myself a limited block of material to examine. The study is not meant to be exhaustive, but merely informative, especially for the purpose of introducing written and nonwritten sources of information about the Biblical world that the reader may not yet know. It is hoped that this end, in a measure, has been accomplished.

Contents

ABBREVIATIONS

The following are used in the notes and in the bibliography.

BA   *Biblical Archaeologist*
JBL   *Journal of Biblical Literature*
ANEP   *The Ancient Near East in Pictures*
ANET   *Ancient Near Eastern Texts Relating to the Bible*
BDB   *A Hebrew and English Lexicon of the Old Testament*, Brown, Driver, Briggs
AP   *Archaeology of Palestine*, W. F. Albright
JPOS   *Journal of Palestine Oriental Society*
AASOR *Annual of the American Society for Oriental Research*
BASOR *Bulletin of the American Society for Oriental Research*
KJV   King James Version of the Bible
RSV   Revised Standard Version of the Bible
BANE   *The Bible and the Ancient Near East*
PEQ   *Palestine Exploration Quarterly*
IEJ   *Israel Exploration Journal*

8

1 A Geographic Survey of the Valley

According to geologists a series of gigantic faults in the crust of the earth brought about the collapse of land which now forms the Jordan Valley. The fault went north on one side and south on the other side, so that today the east side is not parallel in structure nor height with the west side. There are mountain ranges along both sides of the valley. For the most part the eastern mountains are higher with a sharper slope. However, in the north, in the Huleh region, the reverse is true. There on the western side of the valley is a sharp two-thousand-foot scarp. The eastern side has basaltic flows and no walls. South of the Dead Sea basin, which is 2,500 feet below sea level, the earth rises gradually to a height of 650 feet above sea level, and at one hump in the Arabah to 800 feet. This rise creates a water divide in the Arabah, so that flood waters move north into the Dead Sea, and theoretically south toward the Gulf. A series of lateral depressions, however, allows so much water to disappear into the arid land that there is no one channel where all the water can gather to flow south.

The rise begins in the Arabah at the cliffs of Khaneizir; about fifty miles south of these cliffs the valley reaches its highest point at Jebel er-Rishe; there it slopes down again to the Gulf of Aqaba. North of Rishe the valley is wider. The

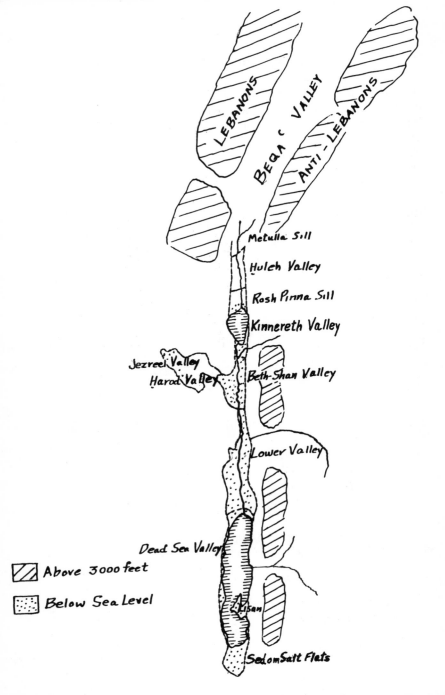

Metulla Sill

Huleh Valley

Rosh Pinna Sill

Kinnereth Valley

Jezreel Valley
Harod Valley

Beth-Shan Valley

Lower Valley

Dead Sea Valley

Lisan

Above 3000 feet

Below Sea Level

Sedom Salt Flats

ALIGNMENT AND REGIONS OF THE JORDAN VALLEY

Ascent of the Scorpions, just north of the Wadi Murra, leads up into the Negev. Routes from the north and south meet the Wadi Murra at a spring called Ein Hosb (thought to be Oboth of Num. 33:43). Across from Ein Hosb there is the ruin of a Nabatean settlement now called Umm et-Teleih, and about twelve miles south of this was the Biblical Punon (modern Feinan) where copper was mined from the Bronze Age to Roman times. Abundant water supply made it possible for the children of Israel to use Punon as one of their encampments as they ended the years of wilderness wandering.[1]

The eastern mountains bordering the Arabah rise to 5,000 feet for many miles in the areas north and south of Petra. Wadi Musa passes through a narrow gorge into the valley city of Petra and out again toward the Arabah. In the Arabah the Nabateans built the sites now called Bir Madhkur and Ein et-Taiyaba as forts to guard the entrance to Petra. The heavy rains from the eastern highlands push soil through diagonal valleys which open into the Arabah, creating great alluvial fans. The water empties into a depression (Wadi Jeibe), flowing north, which like the Jordan has cut into the valley floor anywhere from thirty to one hundred fifty feet. The gravel and sand which wash down across the Arabah create a wide plain known as the Sahl.

South of the Sahl the Arabah narrows down to six miles or less and steep cliffs appear on both sides. On the east granite outcroppings form the mountains of Midian. Alluvial fans may also be seen at the ends of the valleys cutting through the southeastern mountains and, as in the north, the sediment is carried beyond the fans into basins in the Arabah, creating three great mud flats. Near each mud flat is a spring. One, situated very near the Gulf of Aqaba, supplies the modern city of Aqaba with its water. Another spring, some twenty miles north of the Gulf, is called Ein Gharandal, and the third, a full forty miles north of the Gulf, is called Ein Ghudyan. The Wadi Yatm goes through the granite mountains northeast of the Gulf and joins a plain known as the Hasma, which is the gateway to Arabia.

The Dead Sea itself is a deep natural basin with no outlet.

The only way water can leave it is by evaporation, and consequently it continues to grow larger. The northern part of the Sea is very deep (to 1200 feet) but south of the Lisan (a tongue of land which juts out from the eastern side) the water is barely thirty feet deep. It is conjectured that an earthquake allowed the flooding of this shallow area. The continuous rising of the sea may have covered early cities on its shore, perhaps Sodom and Gomorrah.[2] The Dead Sea itself contains about one-fourth to one-third mineral salts which come from mineral springs deep in the earth under the sea and along the valley.[3] As may be expected the entire valley is an area of above-normal earthquake activity, averaging about four earthquakes per century. In 1837 the town of Tiberias was almost wiped out by an earthquake.

The steep mountains on the east of the sea reach right to the edge of the water, leaving no room for a road. On the west the mountains are far enough back for a road, and the oases are neatly spaced so as to provide water along this road. Along the southern third of the eastern side, the cliffs are sufficiently removed from the sea to create a broad, well-watered plain, although the Lisan itself, which juts out to within two miles of the western side, is nothing but lime marl. This broad plain is fed enough water the year around to provide grain, dates, and grapes, which at times have been shipped by boat across the sea. The Old Testament gives no evidence of travel by boat on the Dead Sea. But we see ships plying the sea on the Madaba Mosaic Map (see Chapter 6), which would reflect the situation in Roman times. South of the sea is the Sebkha, a salt marsh where the wadies lose themselves. Adjoining this region and abutting the southwest side of the Dead Sea is Jebel Usdum (Mount Sodom), a fantastic mountain of salt six miles long and over six hundred feet high.

The western slopes of the valley adjacent to the Dead Sea are part of the wilderness of Judea. This desert is created

The Dead Sea, looking toward the Lisan and the mountains of Moab.

Ein-es-Sultan spring near Old Testament Jericho.

because of the leeward exposure and the steepness of these mountains. Moist warm air from the Mediterranean drops its water as it rises and cools over the western slopes. This air is warmed again as it passes over the valley and therefore holds its moisture until it reaches the mountains of Moab. Underground springs like Ein es-Sultan at Jericho, Ein Feshkha near Qumran and En-gedi about twenty miles south of Qumran create oases; otherwise the leeward slopes in this region are usually barren. During the winter months a combination of climatic conditions can bring an occasional torrential rain to the Jordan Valley and to the western slopes, so that for a brief period in the spring green appears. On the eastern side of the Jordan Valley the highland facing west catches and condenses the moisture that is left in the western winds. As a result numerous perennial streams (wadies) empty water into the Jordan and the Dead Sea. There is more surface water on the eastern side of the valley.

Moving north of the Sea of Galilee we come to the point generally considered the beginning of the Jordan Valley, at the town called Metulla. A frontier village between Israel and Lebanon, this town is at the southern edge of an irrigated

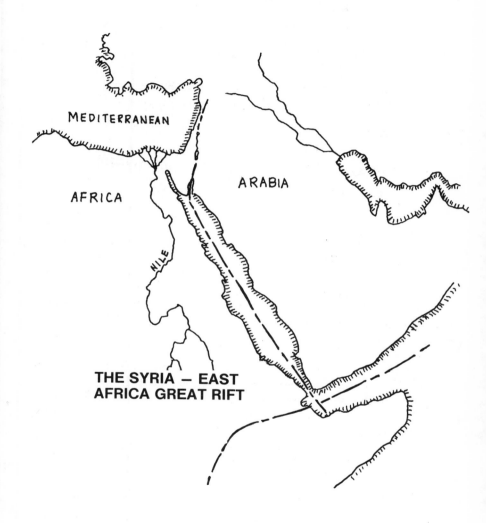

MEDITERRANEAN

AFRICA

NILE

ARABIA

**THE SYRIA — EAST
AFRICA GREAT RIFT**

plain called El Marj, the Town of Marj-ayoun being at the northern end of the plain. The plain is a distinct junction of two of the major segments of the Great Rift Valley which extends from Lebanon to east Africa. The northern segment is a single depression between the Lebanon and the Anti-Lebanon Mountains which creates a long and wide valley 3,000 feet above sea level. This high valley has a northeast-southwest alignment. The other segment is the doublefaulted Jordan rift, which is mostly below sea level and is aligned due north and south.

The first distinct feature of the Jordan Valley is the Huleh area, a depression about three by nine miles culminating, until recently, in a marsh and a shallow lake created by a dam of natural rock. The Huleh region is not really a basin in the same sense as the Sea of Galilee and the Dead Sea, but came about as a result of an ancient lava flow from the east which blocked the water like a moraine lake in glacial country. To remove the lake man needed only to remove the bottleneck. By doing this the Israelis have changed the Huleh Valley from a malarial marsh into a rich farm land and a natural preserve for fauna and flora.

In a sudden descent from about 1600 feet above sea level at Marj-ayoun to 230 feet below sea level in the Huleh region two small western source streams, Nahr Bareighit and Nahr Hasbani, pour their water into the valley. But the two eastern sources of the Jordan provide the major volume of water. They flow out of the ground as sizable streams on the slopes of Mount Hermon. The Liddani appears at Tell el-Qadi, the site of ancient Dan, the northernmost city of ancient Israel (formerly Laish, Judg. 18:7, 27). The Banyasi originates farther up the slope at a village called Banias (Panias), an age-old center of pagan worship which came to be identified with the worship of the Roman god, Pan.[4] Philip the Tetrarch enlarged this town and called it Caesarea (Philippi) in honor of his patron, Augustus Caesar. Three of these headwater streams meet about two miles south of Dan and then divide again to enter the Huleh region as two streams, the Turan and the Jordan.

The Liddani River, a source of the Jordan.

On a plateau overlooking the Huleh plain stands the great Canaanite city of Hazor (Tell el-Qedah). The Jordan alone flows out of Huleh for two miles to "the Bridge of the Daughters of Jacob," where the road between Galilee and Damascus crosses it. After this the Jordan enters a gorge and flows vigorously until it leaves these walls and enters the Sea of Galilee at about 650 feet below sea level. The Sea of Galilee is really a lake formed by a deep basin and is surrounded almost completely by hills. Here and there these hills are withdrawn, creating some plains like the famous plain of Gennesaret (Mark 6:53)[5] in the northwest near Capernaum. The hill country of Galilee can be cold and snowy in the winter, but at the lake shore at nearly seven hundred feet below sea level it is perpetually summer.

From very early times cities were built along the shore. Khirbet Kerak on the southern shore was there long before Abraham entered the land (see Chapter 3). Chinnereth was

the major city on the lake in Old Testament times. In New Testament times Capernaum and Magdala were on the north-west shore and Tiberias was built at the foot of the Valley of Robbers by Herod Antipas, who wanted to honor the Roman emperor Tiberias. Under Roman rule some of the cities of the famed alliance of ten urban centers called the Decapolis controlled the northern Jordan Valley. Hippos was on or near the eastern shore of the sea and Scythopolis (the late name for Beth-shan) was at the eastern entrance to the valley of Esdraelon. Gadara (Luke 8:26, 27), now called Umm Qeis, overlooked the juncture of the Jordan River and the river Yarmuk, and Pella (Fahil) was on the edge of the Transjor-danian slope southeast of Scythopolis.

For about twelve miles south of the Sea of Galilee the valley does not exceed a breadth of four miles. At the plain of Beth-shan (Beisan, Beth-shean), it widens to six or seven miles. This plain terraces on the western side toward the level of the Plain of Esdraelon, which spreads all the way to the Mediterranean.

The Jordan River itself is but a groove cut into the bottom of the valley, which is said to be an old sea bed. Its current does not look swift but can be treacherous. The water drops in the north about forty feet per mile, although the average drop is only about nine feet per mile. The formidable barrier created by the river is due to factors other than the width or swiftness of the stream. Indeed, in the north the river is not as great a barrier because the distinct features of the valley are less pronounced there. The valley itself is the real barrier and it consists of three most interesting features called in Arabic the *Ghor* or lowland, the *Qattara* or sterile chalk hills, and the *Zor* or thicket.

The *Ghor* is the valley floor itself, bounded on either side by mountains or high plateaus. Here are layers of cultivable alluvial deposits which need only irrigation to make the *Ghor* rich farmland. The results of such irrigation may be seen today along the eastern side of the *Ghor*, where water is now

The Jordan River as it flows into the Sea of Galilee.

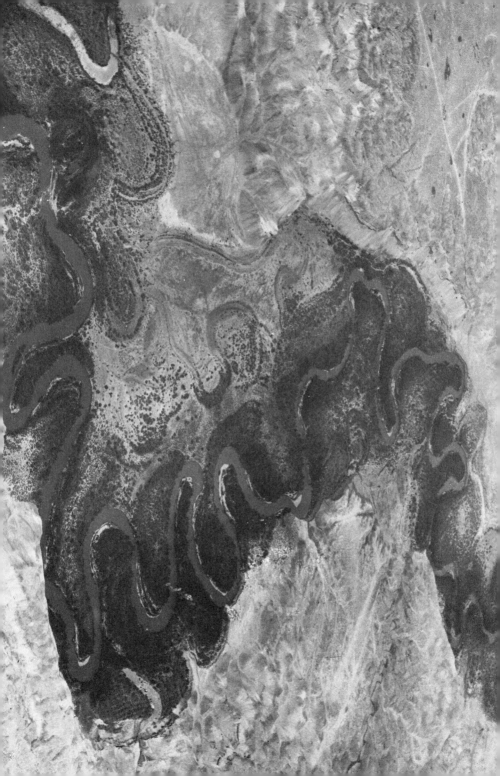

available from the river Yarmuk. Numerous geological faults meet the *Ghor* on both sides, forming valleys, some of which contribute water to the Jordan. On the east side the Jordan has two major tributaries, the Yarmuk and the Jabbok. The Yarmuk, just south of the Sea of Galilee, provides as much water as does the Jordan itself. On the north side of the Yarmuk gorge, some seven or more miles from the confluence, stands the ancient el-Hammeh, a famous hot spring. A high culture flourished here from as early as the fourth millenium B.C. The warm curative waters have been popular throughout history.

About thirteen miles from the Sea of Galilee the river Harod (Jalud) joins from the west, flowing through the plain of Beth-shan. The *Ghor's* seven mile width is constricted again farther south by the hills of Samaria. Even farther south the Wadi Fariah joins from the west to widen the floor again to eight miles, from there it continues to widen to a maximum of fourteen miles at Jericho. A gushing spring called Ein Fariah, at the head of the valley, supplies a rich quantity of water creating a beautiful green valley; but due to irrigation little of this water ever reaches the Jordan. The same is true of Wadi Qelt and Ein es-Sultan, which help create the rich green oasis at Jericho. Irrigation water must come from the sweet water streams before they reach the Jordan, because the Jordan River itself receives mineral salts from numerous springs which make its water increasingly unfit for irrigation.

About one hundred feet below the main valley floor is the depression called in Arabic the *Zor* (the thicket or jungle), through which the Jordan itself flows. The *Zor* can get nearly a mile wide when the river twists upon itself, though the river is only from ninety to a hundred feet wide and ranges from three to twelve feet in depth. The *Zor* contains the river

An airview of the zigzag meanderings of the Jordan River. The darkened areas which surround the twisting river are called the *Zor*. The edge of the valley floor (*Ghor*), bounded by a high plateau, is shown on the upper left.

when it floods in the spring but, unlike the Nile, the Jordan flood is violent, carrying soil away and leaving debris, so that the rank growth which is left is well called the thicket (*Zor*). Jeremiah describes the *Zor* as a jungle: "Behold he shall come up like a lion from the jungle of the Jordan." (Jer. 49:19) The *Zor* provided shelter for lions in ancient times and elephants in pre-historic times and was until very recently the haunt of the wild boar. Due to the twisting, fickle, snakelike route of the Jordan the *Zor* jungle becomes a formidable barrier. The *Qattara* is a badlands area between the *Zor* and the *Ghor* made up of lime marl hillocks. The extent to which the *Qattara* and the *Zor* are developed varies along the course of the Jordan. Nothing can grow in the gray chalky soil of the *Qattara*.

The valley complex affected history as any great geographical barrier would. Not all the ideal tribal boundaries set up by Joshua continued but the Jordan Valley as a boundary served its purpose well. The tribe of Gad had the following Jordan Valley boundary towns: Beth-haram, Beth-nimrah, Succoth and Zaphon (Josh. 13:27, 28). This boundary included the Jordan as a border as far as the lower end of Lake Chinnereth (Galilee). All the land adjacent to the Jordan eastward belonged to Gad. The text of Joshua summarizes the description of the territory by saying: "These are the inheritances which Moses distributed in the plains of Moab adjacent to the Jordan of Jericho, eastward." (Josh. 13:32)[6]

The extent to which the Jordan Valley is a natural border or barrier is also reflected in the incident recorded in Joshua 22, where the people of Reuben, Gad, and half the tribe of Manasseh, after helping the other tribes conquer the land, departed to return to their families east of the Jordan. They stopped in the Jordan Valley before crossing and built a great altar "at the frontier of the land of Canaan, in the environs of the Jordan, alongside the children of Israel."[7] After much persuasion these eastern tribes convinced their brethren that

The lower part of the Jordan Valley, showing the marl hillocks called Qattara.

they had no intention of using the altar for sacrifice but wanted it only as a memorial to remind the children of Israel that the eastern tribes, so near and yet so far, did have a part in the altar at Shiloh. The fear was that in generations to come the inhabitants on the western side of the Jordan would say to the easterners, "What part do you have in the Lord God of Israel, for the Lord has made the Jordan a border between us and you . . . " (v. 25). To guard against this alienation the great altar was erected in the valley as a memorial. It is curiously true that even today a distinct alienation of spirit is often experienced between the Arabs of Palestine and those on the east side of the Jordan. Those in the east feel they are more pure in their bedouin Arab traditions. The Arab-Israeli conflict has made this natural borderland an important political and military front just as it so often was in Biblical days.

1.   A comparison of Numbers 21:4-10 and 33:42-43 leads one to the conclusion that it was here at Punon that the brazen serpent was set up. The Israelites were helped by their friends, the Kenite coppersmiths, to cast the serpent. At the same time the location was sufficiently removed from the highland strongholds of the hostile Edomites.

2.   Dead Sea levels have fallen since 1900, following the rain pattern. PEQ 99:45.

3.   Modern people extract potash from the Dead Sea, the ancients gathered bitumen floating on its surface ("The Nabatean Bitumen Industry at the Dead Sea," BA 22:40-48).

4.   The area was noted for its pagan shrines at Caesarea and Abel-beth-maacah (II Sam. 20:14, 18), and for the idolatry associated with the golden calf at Dan (I Kings 12:29, 30).

5.   Gennesara was the Aramaic designation for this area where a town of the same name was located in Old Testament times. Numbers 34:11 uses the name Chinnereth, which is rendered Ginnesar in the Aramaic translation. A town by this variantly spelled name was evidently located here and gave its name both to the sea (Luke 5:1) and the plain.

6.   See Chapter 2, footnote 12, for a explanation of this translation, especially the use of the word "adjacent." The text has just

described the territory of Reuben, Gad, and half of Manasseh, which was not just "east of Jericho," as in the translations (KJV, RSV). The New English Bible drops "Jericho" without explanation.

7.   Joshua 22:11. Here the English translations have not been satisfactory. The RSV use of "frontier" for *'el mul* and "region" for *'el gᵉlilōt* is good, but the translation of *'el 'ēber* as "on the side that belongs to" is no better than the KJV "at the passage of." The idiom *'el 'ēber* simply means "alongside of." As mentioned in the preceding footnote this usage will be discussed in Chapter 2, footnote 12.

2 The Jordan of Jericho

For centuries the derivation of the term *Jordan* has been a challenge to Hebrew scholars. The most popular explanation derives it from the root *yrd* (descend) as the "river that goes down." But this derivation fails to explain the last letter, not to speak of the vocalization. The Greek form *ho Iardanēs*[1] and the Egyptian *Iarduna*[2] imply that the four letters *yrdn* are part of the root. Some scholars have looked for a non-Hebrew origin. Koehler in his Hebrew lexicon cites von Soden's negative reaction to an Iranian explanation which posits two Indo-European words, *yar*—year and *don*—river, thus the "always flowing river," similar to the meaning of the Sumerian word for the Tigris, *idigna*—"always streaming river."[3] A good explanation is C. H. Gordon's interesting suggestion, based on Homeric references to *ho Iardanos* as rivers in Crete and Elis, that *yardēn* is an East Mediterranean word for "river."[4]

The early Aegean contacts with the Bible world are now more than ever appreciated, as studies in Homer and Minoan documents strengthen the view that the East Mediterranean peoples of the second millenium were interdependent. It is now reasonable to look toward the West as well as toward the East for an understanding of Biblical terminology. C. H. Gordon points out regarding Genesis 10 that ". . . the very first group is the Japhethite branch including the Ionians and the inhabitants of Cyprus and the islands of the Aegean (vv. 2-5). . . . When the Hebrews themselves see fit to place the populations of the East Mediterranean at the very head of the list, we may safely conclude that the area was of prime importance in the Bible world."[5] In the Bible from the patriarchal times on we find not only the East Mediterranean Philistines, who bequeathed their name to the land of Palestine, but also their cousins, the Cretim and the Caphtorim, who are mentioned in Egyptian and Ugaritic sources.[6] It is also well established that some Hebrew common nouns have an Aegean origin.[7] These sea peoples played a significant role in the cultural continuum throughout the East Mediterranean littoral from the early second millenium.[8] Jerome suggested that the "Jor" of Jordan was from *ye'ōr* (stream, used of the Nile and other rivers) which he says is equivalent to Greek *hreithron* (stream). The second half of Jordan, "dan," he takes as the city Dan near one of the river's sources. While this etymology is highly questionable, it appears that the Homeric usage of *Iardanos* has affinity with the word *hreethra* (streams). It is therefore most interesting that *ho Iardanos* (cf. LXX *ho Iardanēs*) is used in Homer to designate two rivers, one in Crete and the other on the Peloponnesus.

In the *Iliad* (7:135) Nestor recalls his youth when he fought beside the swift flowing Celadon beneath the walls of Pheia about the streams of Jardan, written *Iardanou amphi hreethra*. Pheia was in Elis, a district on the northwestern corner of the Peloponnesus. In the *Odyssey* (3:292) Menelaus, caught in a storm, brings half his ships to Crete, "where the Cydonians dwelt about the streams of Jardan"; again the phrase *Iardano amphi hreethra* is employed. Homer's use of the same expression to describe two different rivers, especially when in the *Iliad* the name of the river is already mentioned, adds weight to the view that *Iardanou amphi hreethra* means "on both sides of the streams of the river," *Iardanos* being an old East Mediterranean word for "river."

Though we are still without an etymology it must be noted

that consistent use of this word in Hebrew with the definite article, *hayyardēn*, marks *yardēn* as a common noun. It is not characteristic of Hebrew to use the definite article with a proper name. The lexicon by Brown, Driver, and Briggs notes this fact with the statement that the Hebrew article is "Never, however (as in Greek e.g. *ho platon*) before true proper names, though it is used with certain terms, chiefly geographical, of which the original appellative sense has not been lost."[9] Thus, *habba'al*—the lord, *haśśaṭan*—the adversary. It is significant that the only two passages where *yardēn* is used without the definite article are poetry. We attribute this to the archaizing tendency of poetry.[10] Hebrew in its early stages did not use the article at all. So despite these two poetic usages of the word, *yardēn* might have been understood by the people as a common noun employing the article to mean "the river."

A most interesting Old Testament usage of *yardēn* is found in a series of passages in Numbers, Joshua, and I Chronicles where we find the expression *yardēn yerēḥō*. For example, in Numbers 33:50 the plains of Moab are located *'al yardēn yerēho*, which most take to mean "by Jordan near Jericho."[11] But several other passages using *yardēn yerēho*, notably Numbers 34:15, Joshua 16:1, 20:8, and I Chronicles 6:78, have made Old Testament scholars question the text. Here the Hebrew expression is *mē'ēber leyardēn yerēho*, which is regularly translated "beyond the Jordan at Jericho" in the RSV. But the territory described is not limited to the region near Jericho and that is why the texts are questioned.

Likewise, Joshua 20:8 locates the eastern cities of refuge from Bezer in the plain of Reuben to Ramoth in Gilead and Golan in Bashan as adjacent to *(mē'ēber)* the Jordan at Jericho (cf. also I Chron. 6:78). How could all this territory possibly be opposite Jericho? At this point the problem centers around the two words in juxtaposition, *yardēn yerēḥō*. In the three passages, Numbers 34:15, Joshua 20:8, and I Chronicles 6:78, the Hebrew text is identical *(mē'ēber yardēn yerēḥō)* and the Alexandrinus Septuagint of Joshua 20:8 has *peran tou Iordanou Iericho*. But in Numbers

34:15 the Septuagint translators struggled with the meaning and saw fit to add *kata* (toward, by) between *Iordanou* and *Iericho*, as we also have in our English versions. On Numbers 34:15, G. B. Gray in the *International Critical Commentary* says, " 'at Jericho' is an unsuitable limitation in describing the frontier line of two or two and one-half tribes: The phrase has perhaps been mechanically written or added under the influence of Chapter 22:1 and other passages where the limitation is suitably used." *The Interpreter's Bible*, following this lead, says, "The sentence is written as from Canaan itself, for Jericho is said to be eastward,[12] and the mention of Jericho is not exactly a full description of the territory asked for by the tribes of Reuben and Gad."

It is difficult to believe that all these references to *yardēn yerēḥō* were "mechanically written." In my opinion the evidence converges on the point that *yardēn yerēḥō* means exactly what it says in Hebrew: "the river (or Jordan) of Jericho," as distinguished from other Jordans (rivers). Jericho, being one of the world's oldest cities and for so long a time the most commanding fortress in that valley, was employed in this old appellative for the river in days when the root meaning of *yardēn* as "river" was widely understood.

Thus Joshua 16:1 makes sense and may be translated: "The lot of the children of Joseph went out from the 'river of Jericho,' east of the waters of Jericho, going up through the wilderness from Jericho to the hill country of Bethel." Here "the river of Jericho" (*yardēn yereḥo*) refers to the whole eastern border of Ephraim and Manasseh, while "the waters of Jericho" may be a specific reference to Ein es-Sultan, the spring at Jericho. The southern boundary began at the Jordan and went by Jericho up through the barren slopes to Bethel.

I Chronicles 6:78, giving the eastern cities of refuge, would read as follows: "And opposite the river (*yardēn*) of Jericho, that is, on the east side of the river (*yardēn*) . . ."

Numbers 34:15 would read: "The two and a half tribes took their inheritance adjacent to the river (*yardēn*) of Jericho, eastward toward the sunrising."[13]

Since the Jordan Valley was the earliest area in Palestine to have an established urban settlement, some consideration should be given to the notion that this was the "river of the moon (god)" in very early times. If names mean anything, Jericho in the south and the Beth Yerah (Khirbet Kerak) in the north, where the river Jordan leaves the Lake of Galilee, were originally "moon" cities. Their names being derived from the Canaanite word for "moon" (*yerah*) may indicate that they were great centers of moon worship. The Canaanites also worshiped the moon at Hazor farther north on the edge of the Huleh valley.[14] A term such as *yardēn yerēh(o)* (the river of the moon) may be behind the terminology dealt with in the passages above.

1. As in the Septuagint.

2. ANET, p. 242, as taken from J. Simons, *Handbook for the Study of Egyptian Topographical Lists Relating to Western Asia* (Leiden, 1937).

3. Koehler-Baumgartner, *Lexicon in Veteris Testamenti Libros.*

4. Cyrus H. Gordon, *World of the Old Testament*, p. 122, n. 19; Koehler-Baumgartner also notes this link, citing *Realenzyklopaedie der klassischen Altertumswissenschaft, in loco.*

5. *New Horizons in Old Testament Literature*, p. 21.

6. Cf. Genesis 10:13, 14; Deuteronomy 2:23; Amos 9:7; II Samuel 8:18; Ezekiel 25:16; Zephaniah 2:5; ANET, p. 241, n. 39; Cyrus H. Gordon, *Ugarit and Minoan Crete*, pp. 28, 30, 49 n. 10.

7. The words *kōba'* (helmet) *seren* (lord) and possibly *hᵃdōm* (footstool) are loan words from the sea people.

8. Gordon, *Ugarit and Minoan Crete*, p. 14.

9. BDB, p. 207, 1a.

10. The two passages are Psalm 42:7, and Job 40:23. Poetry in any language tends to preserve archaic grammar. So even a common noun which otherwise might carry an article, in old Hebrew poetry would fail to have it.

11. "At Jericho" (RSV); "near Jericho" (KJV).

12. In numerous places where *'ēber* (usually translated "beyond" or "opposite") is used in relation to the Jordan the author specifies which side he means. Thus Joshua 1:5 speaks of the west, but Numbers 34:15 explicitly speaks of the east. *'Ēber* itself simply means "a side" or just "opposite" or "adjacent" and has no reference to which side. For example, in Exodus 32:15 the tablets

of the law were written *miššnê 'ebrēhem*, "on both their sides." The force of *'ēber* as "adjacent to" or "opposite" reminds us of the New Testament use of the preposition *peran* in the phrase translated "Bethany beyond Jordan." The Greek phrase says nothing about which side Bethany was on. *Peran*, when not used with verbs of motion, denotes "across from," "opposite" or "over against" (Cf. Pierson Parker, "Bethany beyond Jordan," JBL [December 1955]). This also explains the Matthew 4:15 quotation from Isaiah 9:1, 2, where Galilee seems to be placed "beyond Jordan;" both the Old and New Testaments should be translated "over against (adjacent to) the Jordan in Galilee of the Gentiles." This also dissolves the old notion that Jericho was being considered east of the writer while he was pretending to be Moses in Transjordan.

13. The city of Jabesh (Gilead) either gave its name to or received its name from the Wadi Yabis. Compare: Nahr el-Leddani (the Dan stream) and the city of Dan.

14. Cf. Yigael Yadin, *Hazor* 1:89.

3 Prehistoric Times and the Early Bronze Age

The terminology "the Jordan of Jericho" (see Chapter 2) suggests a limitation of the valley to the lowland between the Lake of Galilee and the Dead Sea. But the Arabah, south to the Gulf of Aqaba, and the area around the Lake of Galilee north to the sources of the Jordan should be included in any consideration of the Jordan Valley. Moreover, we must of necessity begin any such consideration in prehistoric times because archaeology has shed so much light on these earlier periods that to ignore it would only obscure the Biblical picture. For a fuller understanding we recommend *Palestine Before the Hebrews* by E. Ananti.

The Jordan Valley was one of the earliest areas in the world to have an established urban settlement, and as far as our present knowledge goes, Jericho was the major prehistoric settlement in the valley. Thanks to the excavations of Kathleen Kenyon, information on Jericho back to Neolithic times has been greatly expanded.[1] This particular valley site was chosen because it is watered by Wadi Qelt and has been provided from time immemorial with just about the best spring in the valley, now called Ein es-Sultan. Natufian people like those who lived in caves near Mount Carmel were already in Jericho in Mesolithic times. The last of their wooden structures was burned about 7800 B.C. ± 210 years, if the carbon 14 dating of this charcoal is correct. After considerable time, perhaps hundreds of years, there developed curious round houses made of hand-molded plano-convex bricks. Kenyon believes that this first urban settlement had direct links with the Natufian hunters and therefore presents to archaeologists a striking example of the transition of man from hunter to city dweller. This pre-pottery-Neolithic culture expanded rather quickly into a highly developed city with great defenses, including a wall six feet, six inches thick and a great stone tower which still stands in ruins thirty feet high. Kenyon dates the tower and wall to about 7000 B.C. If Kenyon's dating is correct, the great village antedates other early city complexes by over two thousand years, and is an example of monumental architecture four thousand years before the pyramids of Egypt. Kenyon infers from all this that there was also a sophisticated system of agriculture based on irrigation which used the water always available at Jericho. Such a system implies strong central control, hence the great city.

After some centuries of abandonment Jericho was rebuilt by a Tahunian people who used a different type of flint implement but are most noted for large houses with many rooms, and walls made of cigar-shaped, thumb-printed bricks. The floors were carefully laid, lime-surfaced and painted. One shrine had a portico supported by six wooden posts, where phallus models indicate that some kind of fertility cult was already in practice. Other artifacts included clay statues of family units and animal figurines, possibly idols. But most curious of all was a "school" of plastic art, a technique of overlaying human skulls with clay features and using shell inlays for eyes. They probably used the plastered skulls in ancestor worship, as the Romans originally used busts of their ancestors. Despite all this artistic ability in plaster these people still were without clay pottery, using finely worked stone bowls instead.

About 5000 B.C. a new people arrived in Jericho. They had fire-hardened pottery but a culture inferior to that of the Tahunian. A flint industry continued, and also a form of

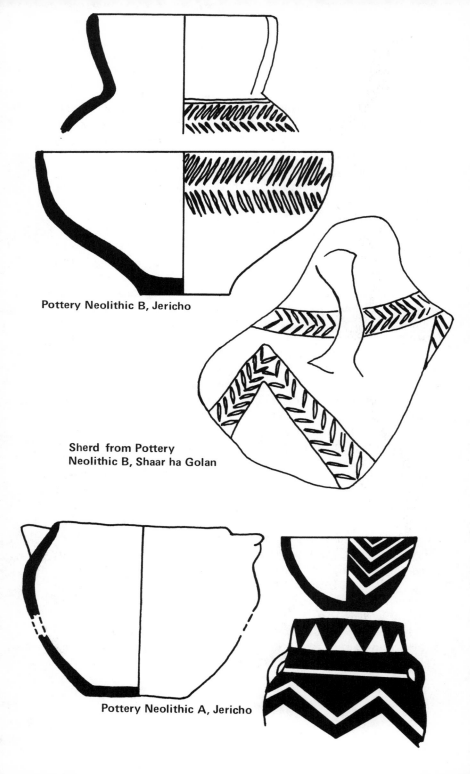

Pottery Neolithic B, Jericho

Sherd from Pottery
Neolithic B, Shaar ha Golan

Pottery Neolithic A, Jericho

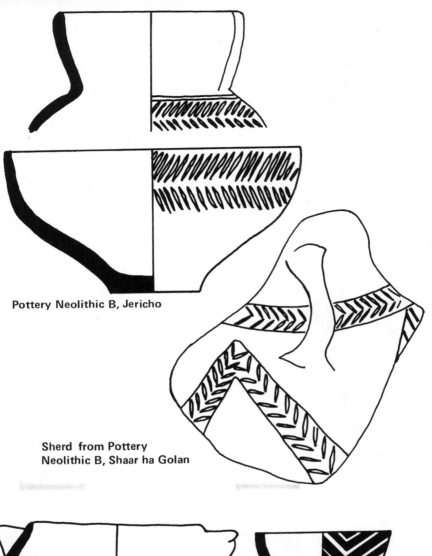

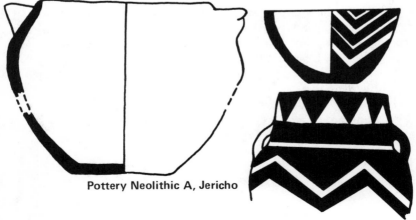

Pottery Neolithic A, Jericho

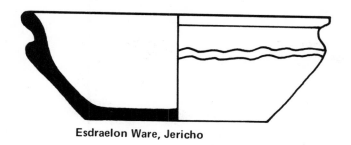

Esdraelon Ware, Jericho

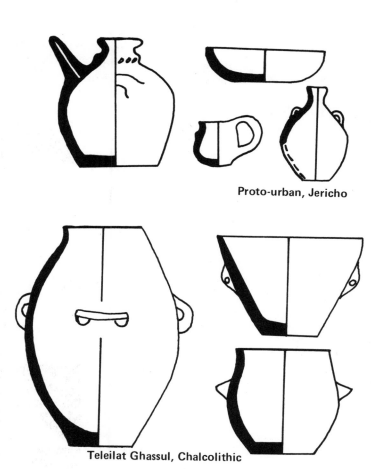

Proto-urban, Jericho

Teleilat Ghassul, Chalcolithic

NEOLITHIC AND CHALCOLITHIC POTTERY FROM THE JORDAN VALLEY

plastic art in which lime-marl was smeared on a framework of reeds to create a flattened human head sporting large inlaid shell eyes, prominent eyebrows, and cheekbones with painted lines depicting hair and beard. At first the people were pit-dwellers whose only real contribution to civilization was a rare red on cream pottery and a somewhat coarse flint. A later phase of this incursion included new people who began to build huts over the pits of their predecessors and eventually built houses and stone walls. They also developed a better fired pottery which was thinner and contained less straw, and often had a herringbone design. For the first time ties with pottery from other sites like far-away Byblos become evident. Kenyon is convinced of a definite relationship between this pottery-Neolithic B culture of Jericho and a Jordan Valley site at the junction of the Yarmuk now bearing the Hebrew name Shaar ha-Golan. Here great quantities of pottery, flint, and animal bones were discovered accidentally during the digging of an anti-tank ditch. The pottery-Neolithic culture found at Jericho existed throughout the northern Fertile Crescent. It was a distinct cultural retrogression from pre-pottery Jericho with its mammoth architecture. Apart from the broad fact that the pre-pottery people of Jericho had a Natufian culture, a conclusion drawn from the kind of flints they made, no one has ever satisfactorily explained where they came from or how they arrived at their advanced urban stage.

Further progress came with the introduction of copper in the Chalcolithic period (4500-3200 B.C.). It is best represented in the Jordan Valley at Teleilat Ghassul, located on the east side of the Jordan just north of the Dead Sea. Here in the first half of the fourth millenium an advanced civilization existed which brings us to the dawn of history (3000 B.C.). Jericho was unoccupied while Ghassul flourished. The excavators[2] of Ghassul found three successive cities with houses of sun-dried mud bricks. Their plastered walls bear polychrome frescoes of stylistic animals, birds and geometric designs of the highest quality. Date and olive stones and kernels of grain found in large storage bins point

Excavations at Teleiat Ghassul.

to a long-lasting agricultural community. Irrigation farming in the areas like Ghassul must have existed into the Biblical period, providing food in "the plains of Moab"[3] and other watered areas of the valley. Stone-lined graves at Ghassul give evidence of a belief in the after-life. These people, like the Egyptians, put food, utensils, and even luxuries in graves for use in the afterworld. Since the work of Mallon and Koeppel at Teleilat Ghassul the Ghassulian culture has been identified widely throughout Palestine, at the sea coast, and in the Negev (Tell Abu Matar near Beersheba). But the culture was especially prevalent in the Jordan Valley showing up at Mefjar, Abu Habil, Jiftlik, Beth-shan, En-gedi, and Tell esh-Shuneh just south of the Lake of Galilee.[4]

Perhaps in Neolithic, but more probably in Chalcolithic times, the dolmen builders lived in or near the Jordan Valley. They did not build their dolmens (tombs?) in the floor of the valley itself but along the edge of the valley. The people themselves probably lived in the Jordan Valley. The dolmens are massive slabs of rough-cut stone set up to produce house-like structures.[5] Not much is known about the dolmen builders, but it is assumed that they were farmers

Neolithic tower at Jericho.

and herders whose domain is outlined for us by the thousands of dolmens throughout Syria and Transjordan. One sure thing about them is that they were experienced builders, since they were able to quarry and erect such megaliths for burial purposes, if that was indeed the purpose of these structures.

Prehistoric sites are more common in the Jordan Valley than in the hill country, but the early strata are often so deep that excavators cannot easily reach them. In addition to Jericho two important valley sites which have yielded early data are Tell el-Husn (Beth-shan) and Khirbet Kerak (Beth-yerah) on the west side. On the east side near the juncture of the Jordan and the Jabbok is Khirbet Umm Hamad. We do not even know the ancient name of this tell, for it was abandoned before 3000 B.C. Yet it was a center of civilization, as is revealed by an abundance of pottery sherds from Chalcolithic times and the beginning of the Early Bronze Age (ca. 3200 B.C.). The Early Bronze pottery has a distinctive ledgehandle folded over like the flap of an envelope.[6]

The end of the fourth millenium is called the Proto-urban period by Kenyon. On the basis of tomb pottery, she finds three groups of people coming into Palestine in this period via the Jordan Valley. Their place of origin is as yet unknown. They did not build cities, but lived in unwalled villages. Little is known of their way of life except that they buried their dead in large tombs using the principle of second interment; either removing or piling up the bones of those long dead in order to make room for the recently dead. Similar pottery in the hill country shows that the Jordan Valley was used only as an entrance into Palestine. Some of them came from the north and settled ultimately in the plain of Esdraelon, while others came from the east via Jericho. Kenyon calls this period Proto-urban because it corresponds to the Proto-dynastic in Egypt and the Proto-literate in Mesopotamia. But here in Palestine no great central government developed nor did writing appear. Still a giant step forward was taken in urban development.[7]

City states began to appear with a comparatively high material culture. Trade flourished between Mesopotamia and

Early Bronze Pottery from Jericho.

Egypt with Palestine as the crossroad. Temples appeared at Jericho and in the Esdraelon Valley at Megiddo. G. C. Wright observes that the earliest Egyptian object ever found in Palestine is a slate palette found at Early Bronze Jericho.[8]

Jericho, already an ancient city, had a very checkered history in the Early Bronze period, as indicated by a succession of sixteen Early Bronze walls. This reflects the frequency of earthquakes in the valley. Some of the Early Bronze walls at Jericho have an anti-earthquake design: a series of thick wall sections separated by alternating thin sections made with facing stones only, so that during an earthquake the whole wall would not tumble. But the succession of walls also reflects the struggle between the settled people of the fertile valleys and those of the nearby deserts. At one point invaders left three feet of ashes against the mud brick wall after an attempt to burn the city. Eventually Jericho was completely destroyed about 2300 B.C. and a new culture was introduced.

Beth-shan's earliest settlements go back into the Chalcolithic period. This great fortress commanded the juncture of the valley of Esdraelon and the Jordan Valley. It had a long history and excavation there has been exceedingly fruitful.[9] Two of the most vital discoveries from the early settlements at Beth-shan are the "apsidal" house type (rectangular with one rounded end) and the gray- and black-burnished pottery which some archaeologists call Esdraelon ware. This culture continued in Beth-shan down into the beginning of Early Bronze I (3200-2800 B.C.). Throughout the balance of the Early Bronze Age the city continued as an important Canaanite center, though apparently unwalled.

The town anciently called Beth-yerah (Khirbet Kerak), which means "the temple of the moon (god)," was located near the place where the Jordan leaves the Lake of Galilee. Around 3000 B.C. the pottery of Beth-yerah was decorated with bands of slip, some parallel and others crisscross. Such band-slip ware is typical of the northern pottery culture of Palestine at this time, although a different kind of band-slip ware is found in the south at Jericho and in the hill country. The period marks the beginning of town building outside the valley. Beth-yerah during the Early Bronze I period had a mud-brick wall over twenty feet thick. Beth-yerah must have been one of the most important cities of Palestine in its day, perhaps actually the capital of all northern Palestine, for it covered an area of sixty acres.[10] The site was unoccupied from the seventeenth century down to the third century B.C., which explains why it is not mentioned in the Bible and other sources. Albright thinks the city may have been destroyed by the Hyksos before their entry into Egypt. Both Early Bronze I and Early Bronze II show the influence of the powerful Thinite kings of the Egyptian first dynasty (ca. 2800 B.C.). Beth-yerah in the north, Beth-shan in the center and Jericho in the south were three flourishing cities of the Jordan Valley influenced by Egyptian culture throughout the Early Bronze Age (ca. 3200-2200 B.C.).

In Early Bronze III (ca. 2500-2200 B.C.) new and improved techniques of pottery making were invented, kilns with separate combustion chambers came into use, and there was increased use of the potter's wheel, which resulted in the production of the famed Khirbet Kerak (Beth-yerah) ware. W. F. Albright calls this "some of the most beautiful pottery ever made in Palestine."[11] Found in widely separated places as well as in Jericho and Beth-shan, it is red and black

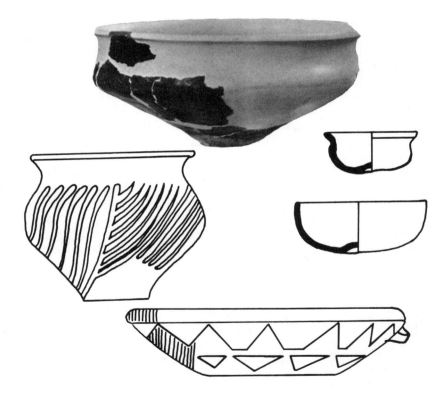

Early Bronze Age Khirbet Kerak ware from Beth-shan.

This burnt ivory bull's head from Early Bronze Age Jericho may be a Mesopotamian import. Another like it was found at Khirbet Kerak.

burnished, beautifully ornamented with geometric designs, sometimes fluted, having a very graceful shape.

Traders brought to Early Bronze Jericho a darkened ivory bull head strikingly similar to work produced by the Sumerians in lower Mesopotamia. But archaeologists agree that Palestine at this time was more strongly under the influence of Egypt. In an Early Bronze II tomb in Beth-yerah there was found a typical stump-based, one-handled Abydos vase very characteristic of First Dynasty Egypt. In the Early Bronze town at Arad, in the eastern Negev overlooking the Jordan Valley, Abydos ware of First Dynasty Egypt was found.[12] More recent excavations at Arad give even greater confirmation to this strong Egyptian presence. For example, the semi-round towers of Early Bronze Arad have been linked with similar towers pictured in Egyptian records of Canaanite towns.[13]

So it was in the Jordan Valley, at the beginning of the third millennium, where self-sufficient villages gave way to city-states which grew to become centers of complex society. There is no evidence of any strong central government at this time in Palestine. In such places as the Jordan Valley and other lowland plains a high and unbroken culture continued down to the end of the Early Bronze Age. Around 2200 B.C. nomads invaded suddenly and destroyed many urban centers like Jericho, Beth-shan and Beth-yerah.

1.   Cf. Kathleen Kenyon, *Digging Up Jericho:* Kenyon, *Excavations at Jericho,* vol. 1; see Chapter two in Kenyon, *Archaeology in the Holy Land.* More recent prehistoric excavations have proceeded in Jordan Valley south of the Sea of Galilee at Munhata (*Révue Biblique,* 75:263-264), Neve Ur (IEJ 17:201-232) and Sheikh Ali (IEJ 9:166-174); in the Huleh valley at Ein Mallaha (IEJ 10:14-22) and Tell Twimus (IEJ 19:65-78); and south of the Dead Sea on the edge of the Arabah at Beidha (PEQ 98:8-72).

2.   Jesuit fathers under the direction of Alexis Mallon and Robert Koeppel excavated the site from 1929 to 1938. See *Teleilat Ghassul, compterendu des fouilles de l'Institut Biblique Pontifical,* vols. 1 and 2 (1934 and 1940). Recent work took place at Ghassul in the winter of 1967 by the British School of Archaeology, to clarify the succession of strata (*Revue Biblique,* April 1968, pp. 247-250).

3.   Located according to the Book of Numbers as near the Jordan: Numbers 22:1; 26:63; 31:12; 33:48-50; 36:13. It was here that the Israelites encamped in a well-watered area before crossing the Jordan.

4.   Cf. G. E. Wright, *The Bible and the Ancient Near East,* p. 81. Abu el-'Alayiq (Herodian Jericho) produced Chalcolithic pottery of a type not found at Ghassul, which has led to positing another culture at a slightly different date, from the Middle Chalcolithic to Early Bronze II, called by Kenyon Proto-urban C. It is one of the three Proto-urban types identified by Kenyon and mentioned below. On other Ghassulian finds see PEQ 99:101, 102 and *The Bulletin of the Israel Exploration Society* 27:1-33.

5.   Excavations at el-'Adeimeh (near Nebo) by Stekelis revealed stone (burial?) cists, thought to be but not necessarily associated with the dolmens (James L. Swauger, "Dolmen Studies in Palestine" BA 29:110), and "Burial Customs and the Dolmen Problem," David Gilead, PEQ 100:16).

6.   W. F. Albright, AP, p. 78.

7.   Kathleen Kenyon, *Archaeology in the Holy Land,* pp. 99-100.

8.   BANE p. 82.

9.   Publications of the Palestine Section of the Museum of the University of Pennsylvania, Vols. 1-4 on Beth-shan (1930-1940).

10. Archaeological work was done at Beth-yerah in April-June 1967 under the direction of D. Ussishkin (*Révue Biblique,* April 1968, pp. 266-268).

11. W. F. Albright, *Archaeology of Palestine,* p. 76.

12. C. F. Pfeiffer, ed., *The Biblical World,* p. 50.

13. The author learned this from personal contact with the excavator, Professor Yohanan Aharoni, in the summer of 1967.

4 Old Testament Times

At the end of the Early Bronze Age there followed a period variously known as the Intermediate Bronze or Middle Bronze I or Early Bronze-Middle Bronze or Early Bronze IV. There is no question but that the people who arrived in the Jordan Valley at this time were completely different from those of the preceding urbanites of the Early Bronze. They appear to be responsible for the destruction of all the major cities of the Jordan Valley: Beth-shan (Beth-shean), Beth-yerah, Tell esh-Shuneh, and Jericho. The culture did not develop out of Palestinian traditions but seems to have had contact with inland Syria, exhibiting a 'caliciform' pottery, new copper weapons, and single burials. Albright, Kenyon, and De Vaux believe these people represent the "Amorite' invasion of which Abraham was a part. There may be a valid tradition behind Ezekiel's derisive statement to the nation, "Thy father as an Amorite . . . " (Ezek. 16:3, 45). In any case it is clear that a people called in Mesopotamian documents "Amurru" (westerners) were on the move at this time. But it may be that the people of the "caliciform" culture who entered Palestine at the end of the Early Bronze Age should not be identified as northwest Semitic Amorites; they may have been only a part of a vast general irruption going on from the twenty-fourth to the twentieth centuries B.C.

45

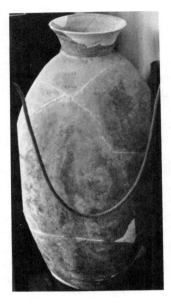

Caliciform-type storage jar from about 2000 B. C.

Mesopotamian documents attest to the presence of a non-Semitic people in the Intermediate Bronze period who had a metallurgic background. Certain dagger tombs of Jericho bear witness to them. Egyptian portrayals of these non-Semites appear in monuments before the twentieth century, though the dominant people of the Jordan Valley were still Semites. Paul W. Lapp offers evidence from his excavations of Bab-edh-Dhra and the Dhahr Mirzbaneh tombs that these non-Semitic metal-bringing people first appeared in the Jordan Valley and Palestine as early as the twenty-fourth century. Indeed, they appeared in Byblos and Ras Shamra as well and seem to be involved in the general upheaval of urban culture and probably the fall of the Old Kingdom in Egypt which was followed by the anarchy of Egypt's first Intermediate Age.

Lapp suggests that the non-Semitic people are related to the Beaker race known from the Western Mediterranean area and Europe, who may have originally come from Central Asia. Their shaft tombs and "caliciform" pottery are found in all the Mediterranean lands, Anatolia, the Aegean, Sicily, Sardinia, and Spain. The people are known for their beer cups (hence "beakers") and metallurgy. They might even be the progenitors of the "Philistines" of the Book of Genesis. Lapp suggests they may be the Perizzites mentioned in Genesis 13:7 and 34:30. These passages suggest to him that the two major groups in the land of Palestine when Abraham arrived were the Canaanites and Perizzites. In Genesis 34:30 Jacob complains that his sons Simeon and Levi have made him "odious to the inhabitants of the land, the Canaanites and the Perizzites." If the Perizzites were indeed these non-Semitic invaders, their name, meaning hamlet-dwellers or peasants, would indicate they were rural people who lived in the open country. The archaeological evidence bears this out, for their architecture is either absent or of a low quality.[1]

In the twentieth century a new group from coastal Syria arrived, bringing pottery similar to that found at Byblos, made on a fast wheel and of high quality. Undoubtedly this was the "Canaanite" element in the society Abraham met when he entered Palestine. He borrowed not only the material aspects of their culture but their language as well. It was a culture that continued without interruption in Palestine down through the Middle and Late Bronze Ages.

The Patriarchal Period

The beginning of Middle Bronze Age corresponds roughly to Old Testament patriarchal times (ca. 2000 B.C.). Genesis 13 and 14 give important evidence of this age in the Jordan Valley. Sites like Khirbet Umm Hamad Gharbi have led Nelson Glueck to the contention that the Jordan Valley was heavily populated between 2100-1900 B.C.[2] Even later than 1900, when Transjordan is thought to have been still largely nomadic, both the Jordan Valley and Western Palestine became more intensively settled. Not only pottery remains but also the Egyptian Execration Texts of the nineteenth and eighteenth centuries point in this direction. Cities like Pella, Hazor, and Rehob along or in the Jordan Valley are named in these documents as foes of twelfth and thirteenth dynasties of Egypt.[3] The Execration Texts are linked also with the fourteenth chapter of Genesis by the occurrence of the unique word *ḥānîk* for Abraham's three hundred eighteen "retainers" (Gen. 14:14). In the Egyptian texts this word describes the soldiers of the Semitic chieftains who are being execrated. The ceremony involved breaking the bases or statuettes inscribed with the names of the king's enemies to assure magically their ultimate destruction.

There was always a considerable population potential on the eastern side of the valley floor because of a dozen perennial tributaries to Jordan. A number of these wadies (Nimrin, Kafrein and Udheimi) water "the plains of Moab" where the Israelites encamped before crossing the Jordan (Num. 22:1). Some have held that Sodom and Gomorrah were in this region north of the Dead Sea, but the evidence seems to be in favor of a southeasterly location. [4] Apparently Lot and Abraham stood in the hill country near Bethel where they could see "the plain of the Jordan that it was well watered everywhere" (Gen. 13:10). Later when the cities of the plain were destroyed Abraham saw the smoke of Sodom from the highlands at Hebron (Gen. 19:28). This would have been equally possible whether the condemned cities were on the northern or southern end of the sea. On the southeastern end of the Dead Sea below the Lisan (tongue) there are cultivated fields and orchards which result from the five streams flowing from the highlands of Moab. Albright has attempted to show that the three main streams of this area provide possible locations for Sodom, Gomorrah, and Zoar. Early church records[5] attest the use of the name *Zoar* until Byzantine times for the area southeast of the Dead Sea, and the salt mountain to the southwest of the sea is still called Jebel Usdum (Mount Sodom).

When W. F. Albright uncovered the cemetery east of the Lisan, at Bab-edh-Dhra, some five hundred feet above the valley floor and about five miles from the Dead Sea, there was

Submerged trees near Jebel Usdum.

what appeared to be a fortress with a religious shrine in the
form of sacred cult pillars.[6] In 1965 Paul Lapp excavated
again at edh-Dhra and found a town with heavy stone fortifications like those of Early Bronze Palestine. This town was
destroyed about 2300 B.C. and was never rebuilt. Its tombs

go back to the earliest phase of the Early Bronze. Many types of tombs (shaft tombs, tholos tombs charnal houses) are attested throughout the Early Bronze period but at the end of this period an entirely new type of burial and pottery appears. This change must represent at least one phase of the newcomers of the Intermediate Bronze Age who brought an end to urban culture of the area. But Abraham and Lot found the Jordan plain to be an area dotted with urban centers. It appears then that Abraham's cities of the plain must be put down at least to the end of the Intermediate Bronze Age, with the patriarchal period being really in Middle Bronze, which was a time of great urbanization in Palestine.

If the remains of Sodom and Gomorrah were in this area they may now be under the waters of the Dead Sea, which has risen and fallen through the centuries, depending on how much water the rivers bring. Water can leave the lake only by evaporation. Trees which once thrived near the water's edge are now dead stumps covered with water and encrusted with mineral salts. Orni and Efrat, in their work, *Geography of Israel*, suggest that tectonic movements at the bottom of the sea influence the water level (p. 82). E. G. Kraeling does not believe that these cities were innundated by the salty waters. He reasons that as the cities were connected with agriculture they would have been on higher ground back from the lake along the five sweet-water streams, perhaps one stream for each of the five cities of Genesis 14:1. Kraeling even suggests a site on one of the hills near the Tell el-Feifeh. But until further investigation establishes the exact place of the ruins of the cities, their location must remain a conjecture. One hardly can take seriously Kraeling's notion that a smelting furnace found in this area gave rise to the Biblical story of the destruction of the cities.[7] It is more likely that a combination of geological and meteorological events not only left the cities in ruins but also eventually covered them with water. Geologists believe the shallow southern basin of the lake was created in the historic past (since 3000 B.C.). Minerals tend to reach the saturation point, recrystallize, sink to the bottom and obscure any evidence of what may have existed on the land now covered by the southern basin.[8]

Abraham came into Palestine in the beginning of the Middle Bronze Age. Reurbanization had already begun. Jericho played no role in Abraham's narrative because it was not yet rebuilt into the great walled city it would become later in this period. Other cities were flourishing, especially in the Jordan Valley.

Abraham was a pastoralist who settled in the hill country while the agriculturalists occupied well-watered areas in the valley plains and built their towns nearby. The five cities of the Vale of Siddim in Genesis 14 were rich cultural centers. Because of their affluence they faced the oppressive yoke of their would-be masters as far away as Mesopotamia, called the land of Shinar.[9] Another well-watered area adjacent to the Dead Sea which interested these oppressors was Hazazon-tamar (Gen. 14:7), which II Chronicles 20:2 identifies with En-gedi (I Sam. 23:29; 24:1), a lush oasis in the midst of the barren Judean wilderness at exactly thirty-one degrees and twenty-nine minutes latitude. Hazazon-tamar means "the cutting of the palm," signifying the fullness for this gushing spring with its waterfalls and pools only a few minutes' walk from the saline waters of the Dead Sea.[10]

It may be also that the four kings of the east were interested in the cities of the Vale of Siddim primarily because of the copper-rich soil not far away. Smelting furnaces stood in the immediate vicinity, and farther south in the Arabah there existed an important copper mining region in the Middle Bronze Age (pp.

The greatest political event of this era was the conquest of northern Egypt by a people the Egyptians called *heqau khasut* (Hyksos), "rulers of foreign countries." With the introduction of the horse and chariot and a new kind of bow, a composite bow made with layers of wood, sinew, and horn glued together, these Hyksos brought havoc not only to Egypt but throughout Palestine and Syria as well. The Jordan Valley city of Khirbet Kerak (Beth-yerah) was destroyed by them as was Jericho. The invaders also entered the hills and conquered and rebuilt numerous towns there. The Hyksos left distinctive material remains but no written records. Even though they controlled northern Egypt for several centuries the only written records of them come later. The Egyptians who never wrote about national humiliations, finally drove out the Hyksos and then mentioned them in appropriate derogatory terms, calling them wretches and miserable Asiatics.[11]

Middle Bronze Jericho presents one of the best examples of Hyksos culture and fortifications. It was enclosed by a brick wall about six feet thick, similar to the town walls of the Early Bronze Age, and built on top of a great plastered rampart. At the foot of the slope another stone revetment wall supported the rampart, creating a great defense system which was bigger than any Jericho had or would ever have again.[12] With both rampart and wall the whole defense system was nearly fifty feet high. Other Palestinian cities also used this "defense in depth" method. It was a system which was common in Palestine and Syria even before the mid-eighteenth century B.C.[13] but was greatly improved by the Hyksos.

The Middle Bronze Age (ca. 1900-1550) was a time when many different ethnic groups were on the move but a unified pottery culture continued throughout Palestine. On the east side of Tell es-Sultan, Kenyon found quantities of loom weights for an extensive weaving industry, tools for flour milling, and even drains beneath the streets. In the tombs west and north of the tell there were communal burials with food and equipment for the after-life. In some of these well-sealed tombs it appears that volcanic gases killed the microbes needed for decomposition, resulting in the preservation of perishable materials such as wooden furniture. This was an unusual discovery for Palestine of Middle Bronze Age. The furniture was simple but of a refined Egyptian design. Miss Kenyon observes:

> These tombs have therefore preserved for us for about 3500 years wooden objects from five-foot tables to boxes an inch or so high, rush baskets and mats, fragments of textiles, and even

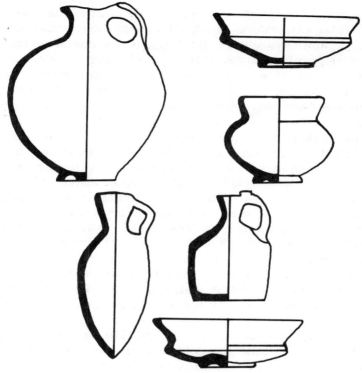

Middle Bronze pottery from Jericho.

portions of flesh and human brains. This is wholly unprece-
dented in Palestine . . . Professor Zeuner's view is that some-
thing has killed the organisms of decay before they had
finished their work.[14]

Domination of the Jordan Valley and Palestine by New Kingdom Egypt

In the century or so immediately before Israel's entry
through the Jordan Valley on the western bank of the Jordan, Egypt had strong control of the land both culturally and
politically. At least a century before the arrival of Israel, a
Semite with the Egyptian name Rewashsha was prince over

the city of Taanach in the valley of Esdraelon. In his correspondence with Egypt, the Egyptian king showed interest in
Rewashsha's Canaanite religion by requesting an omen from
the diviners of the goddess Asherah.[15] Though Hyksos control was gone, an eclectic culture continued in New Kingdom
Egypt. After the arrival of Thutmose III in Upper Retenu
(northern Palestine) and especially after his occupation of
Megiddo in 1468, his scarabs begin to be found in the Jordan
Valley at Beth-shan. Thutmose III and some of his successors
had the habit of listing on their temple walls the names of
countries and city-states over which they had suzerainty.
Although sometimes identifications are difficult the following names from these lists suggest important Jordan Valley
sites: Beth-shan, Chinnereth, Hazor, Pella (Pahel), and
Yanoam. From the time of Sheshonk I a place called Jordan
is found among the lists.[16] It is likely but not certain that
this is a reference to the Jordan Valley.

The Egyptians were not satisfied to drive the Hyksos from
their borders; they followed them, destroying their Palestinian cities swiftly and vigorously, ushering in an age of
military imperialism. Thutmose III was the leading figure.
Hyksos Jericho was destroyed but what followed at Jericho is
an enigma from the archaeological knowledge at hand. It
apparently fell into disuse for some time. The few things
found at Jericho do not include the bichrome ware so prevalent in Palestine at the beginning of the Late Bronze Age.

Beth-shan, on the other hand, was immediately made into
an Egyptian fortress[17] which was destroyed twice before the
end of the thirteenth century. Hazor became a great city with
its Hyksos type "enclosure" filled with dwellings. It too was
destroyed at the close of the thirteenth century. The remains
of the two cities, Beth-shan and Hazor, show clearly the two
phases of the second part of the Late Bronze Age, the
Amarna period and the Ramesside period.

An Amarna letter written by the king of Jerusalem, 'Abdu-
Hepa, to Amenhotep III (1390-1353) speaks of a native
garrison at Beth-shan set up by Tagu, a local prince in the
Carmel area. 'Abdu-Hepa accuses the prince of revolting

against Egyptian authority centered at the coastal city of Gaza.[18] In a somewhat later letter to Akhnaton (Amenhotep IV) 'Abdu-Hepa complains bitterly that the 'Apiru are warring against him and that he needs garrison troops if he is to save the domains of the king.[19] Another Amarna letter was written by Mut-baalu (Man of Baal), the prince of the Jordan Valley city of Pella, to one Yanhamu, a high Egyptian official with a Semitic name. Mut-baalu tells about the defection of nearby cities in the land of Garu (southern Golan region adjacent to the Sea of Galilee). Only the city of Ashtaru (Biblical Ashtaroth, Gen. 14:5; Deut. 1:4; Josh. 13:12, 31) had come to the aid of Mut-baalu of Pella.[20]

The cultural revolution of Akhnaton (Amenhotep IV) hastened the decline of Egyptian political control over Palestine. Cities in Galilee, Carmel, and in the Jordan Valley were throwing off the Egyptian yoke. Even places like Jerusalem and Pella, though still ostensibly loyal to Egypt, were feeling the anarchy resulting from her comparative political weakness or at least indifference in the Amarna Age (ca. 1400).

Scholars are by no means agreed that these 'Apiru of the Amarna letters are the Hebrews, but most agree that the Hebrews could have been identified as 'Apiru, a term for a class of people, not an ethnic group. Similarity between the names may have been coincidental. The 'Apiru appeared in times and at places where there were no Hebrews. It has been noted that in the Old Testament when the Israelites are called Hebrews it is by foreigners (Gen. 39:14, 17; Exod. 2:6; I Sam. 4:6, 9) who might have confused the two names.

Arrival of Israel

Sometime in the Late Bronze Age the Israelites came from Egypt to the Jordan Valley. Pottery offers no evidence of a distinct change of culture from Canaanite to Israelite after Israel arrived in Palestine.[21] We know from the Merneptah Stela that Israel was in Palestine by 1220 B.C., before the Philistine invasion at the beginning of the twelfth century. Yet the Philistines show up first in archaeology with new pottery forms, iron, and unique burial customs, all of which they brought from their homeland somewhere in the east Mediterranean. Such evidence does not contradict the Biblical picture, which presents Israel as an inheritor of a long-standing culture which had roots in Middle Bronze Age Palestine. When Israelite levels begin to appear the major difference is poorer architecture, which might be expected of a people whose seminomadic ways went back hundreds of years. Even in Egypt Israel had been given the land of Goshen, a borderland often inhabited by Semites, because the Egyptians considered themselves superior to the rustic pastoralists (Gen. 46:34).[22]

In their long years of wilderness wandering the Israelites camped at a number of important sites in and near the Arabah. The itineraries of Numbers 21:4-12 and 33:37-45 are said to be contradictory. Y. Aharoni in *The Land of the Bible* views the route in Numbers 33:37-45 to be "the way of the Arabah," by which he means a direct route from Kadesh-barnea to Edom and Moab, a branch of "the king's highway" (pp. 186, 187). If this is so, it is strange that Punon (Feinan) on the east should come before Oboth (Ein el Weibeh) on the west side of the Arabah. Numbers 21:4-12 and Deuteronomy 2:8 insist that Israel went south on the Arabah road toward Ezion-geber and then turned north to the road that led to the wilderness of Moab. It seems unlikely that this tradition, so well established in Hebrew history (Judg. 11:17), would be blandly contradicted. The accounts, to be sure, do not each mention all the same places but the omission, for example, of the Zared River in Numbers 33 certainly does not mean that in this account they did not cross it. We cannot accurately locate enough of the places to trace the route exactly. They were a wandering people and it should be expected that they retraced their steps.

Encampment near Punon (Feinan), a place known for copper production (pp. 11, 24), fits well with the account of Moses' brazen serpent (Num. 21:7-9). The next stop at Oboth may mean that the Israelites descended again into the Arabah valley. Is it necessary to locate the next stop (Num. 33:44

and 21:11), Iye-abarim, at Khirbet 'Ayy southwest of Kerak (Kir-haresheth) as Kraeling suggests (p. 122)? Avi-Yonah prefers to locate Aia (Iye) of the Madaba Map at 'Aine on the north side of the Zared valley (pp. 143-145). If this is Iye-abarim, it is still far enough east to be described as on the eastern frontier of Moab as in Numbers 21:11 and still be considered in the Abarim mountain country.

Israel finally arrived in the Abarim highland north of the Arnon river, a tableland long fought over by the Amorites and Moabites. Before they could move into the Jordan Valley they had to face fierce Amorites who at the time controlled the area just north of the Arnon. Ballad singers in Numbers 21:27-30 celebrated Israel's victory with a bit of political satire. To understand this political satire one must have in mind the people and places of the drama. Heshbon is the modern Hesban situated on a wadi of the same name which lies a little north of thirty-one degrees latitude between Amman and Madaba. The ancient tell has been recently excavated by S. Horn.[23] It was a capital of the Amorites in Moses' day. Sihon, of course, was the Amorite king. Ar was a city on the heights slightly north of the Arnon river. Kemosh was the chief god of the Moabites. Dibon and Madaba were cities north of the Arnon often controlled by the Moabites whose territory was usually south of Arnon. The poem shows the Amorites were strong enough at the time to control the cities south to Ar on the Arnon cleft. The song chides the Amorites, who had recently taken this region from their southern neighbors. The theme is: "You (Amorites) have defeated the Moabites, but we (Israelites) have defeated you."

> Come, let us rebuild Heshbon,
> Let us re-establish Sihon's city.
>
> Fire went out from Hesbon,
> A flame from Sihon's town,
> It devoured the Ar of Moab,
> The citizens on the Arnon heights.
>
> Woe to you, Moab!

You are finished, you people of Kemosh.
Kemosh has surrendered his sons as prisoners,
and his daughters as captives to the Amorite king, Sihon.

But we shot at them; and destroyed Heshbon as far as Dibon;
we ravaged until the fire spread to Madaba.

This battle marked the beginning of Israelite conquest of the land, which required generations and did not come to completion until the time of David.

The Israelites soon controlled a number of Amorite cities north of the Arnon and a few important former Moabite sites. This gave them an opportunity to prepare to enter Palestine via the Jordan Valley. The river itself and the rebuilt city of Jericho were the major obstacles in the way.

The Book of Numbers labels the region at the Jordan across from Jericho, the staging area from which the Israelites made their entry, "the plains of Moab" (Num. 22:1; 25:1; 33:48). Numbers 33:49 gives the north and south extremities of the area of Israel's encampment as Beth-jeshimoth and Abel-shittim respectively. The eastern and western boundaries were the Moabite mountains and the Jordan. Today the area is called Ghor Nimrin and Ghor el-Kefrein, from the names of its two major wadies. Wadi Kefrein joins Wadi Rama to make Abu Gharaba, a perennial stream which enters the Jordan about two miles north of the Dead Sea. Verses 34 and 35 of Numbers 32 mention some towns built (rebuilt) by Israel; among them is Beth-nimrah, believed to be Tell Bleibil. Four miles south of this site is Tell Kefrein, which some take to be Abel-shittim, although Nelson Glueck locates the latter at Tell el-Hammam, nearer the mountains on the same wadi.[24] None of these sites have been excavated and surface sherds go back only to Iron I (1200-900).

About three miles south of Abu Gharaba is Wadi Azeimeh ('Udheimi), a name which preserves in Arabic the same root as the Biblical Beth-jeshimoth (Num. 33:49). Numbers 21:20 says that Moses looked out from the top of Pisgah toward Jeshimon (the wilderness), another form of the same word. The root is also preserved at Khirbet Sweimeh on the Wadi el-Azeimeh and at Tell el-Azeimeh, which guarded the road to the city of Madaba. One of the two must have been Beth-jeshimoth; the latter has the earlier surface sherds. [25] The term Jeshimon implies that the area was barren, and indeed when the rains are not good in the highlands this area of the Jordan Valley can become a barren waste. But when supplied with enough water to keep the wadi and spring flowing, with the help of irrigation the region can become a garden. Such was the case at a very early time, as is known from the excavations at Teleilat Ghassul (p. 36). Balaam had such a situation in mind as he looked out over the Jordan Valley and blessed Israel with these words of Numbers 24:5-7:

> How beautiful are
> your tents, O Jacob,
> your tabernacles, O Israel!
> Like a wadi the Lord, stretched out,
> like a garden beside a river;
> like aloe trees the Lord planted,
> like cedars beside the water.
> Water flows on his irrigated fields
> and his seed has plenty of water.

Israel in the Jordan Valley

Balak, the king of Moab, did not take Israel's presence lightly, though it appears he was in too weakened a condition to drive them away. He turned therefore to exorcism and obtained the services of the diviner Balaam to curse Israel. Balak brought Balaam to three different locations from which he could view Israel spread out in the floor of the valley below. The first of these is called Bamoth-baal (the high place(s) of Baal) in Joshua 13:17 and Numbers 21:19. The famous Moabite Stone (Mesha Inscription) mentions a Beth-bamoth, which some identify with a hill called el-Qweiziyeh about three miles northwest of Madaba and south of Mount Nebo.[26] As for Nebo, King Mesha (830 B.C.), in the Moabite Stone, tells of capturing a town called Nebo from Israel, of slaying seven thousand people, and of dragging

certain religious objects of Yahweh before Chemosh his
god.[27] E. G. Kraeling suggests Nebo in Moses' time may have
been Balak's home town at Kirjath-huzoth (Num. 22:39);
therefore the nearby hilltop at el-Qweiziyeh was the first
place he took Balaam.[28] At this spot one obtains an excellent view of the valley.

Balak also showed Balaam the Israelites in the valley from
a second vantage point on the top of Pisgah (Num. 23:14).
Pisgah itself cannot be identified with any real precision.
Since Joshua 12:3 and Deuteronomy 3:17 mention "the
slopes of the Pisgah" it is usually taken as a sector of the
Abarim range which borders the valley. The term *pisgah* is
always used with the definite article, showing it was an
improper noun, probably meaning "a step or cleft" or some
such natural feature of a mountain. In Deuteronomy 3:17;
4:49; and Joshua 12:3; 13:20 Ashdoth-pisgah means some-
thing like "the slopes of the scarp." The modern Ras Feshka
(Rosh Pisgah) on the northwestern side of the Dead Sea, is a
similar but even more pronounced scarp. That Numbers
23:14 mentions the top of "*the* Pisgah" shows it was one of
the peaks near Mount Nebo. E. G. Kraeling thinks Pisgah is
one of the humps in front of Nebo, because it provides a
good vantage point from which to view the Jeshimon south
of Wadi el-Azeimeh.[29]

Balak finally took Balaam to the top of Peor, which also
overlooks the desert (Num. 23:28). Here Balaam continued
to bless Israel and was finally discharged by a disillusioned
Balak. The place must be the same as Beth-peor (Deut. 3:29;
4:46; 34:6; Josh. 13:20). Balak, who could not get Yahweh
to forsake Israel by exorcism, now devised a plan to get Israel
to forsake Yahweh (Rev. 2:14). It appears that Balak, with
the advice of Balaam, used prostitutes (perhaps temple prostitutes) to entice many Israelites to follow after the Baal of
Peor (Num. 25:1-3; Deut. 4:3), a deity associated with the
temple-town Beth-peor. Some scholars locate Beth-peor behind Mount Nebo at the ruins called Sheikh Jayel, a place
still sacred to bedouin.[30] Eusebius's *Onomasticon* speaks of a
Mount Peor as six Roman miles east of Livias (Tell er-

Rameh).[31] Mount Peor would then be immediately north of
Mount Nebo. From each of these lookout points on a clear
day the Jordan Valley can be viewed for long distances.
Moses viewed the valley and the high country of Palestine
and Gilead to the north from one of the same sites used by
Balaam and was reminded of God's covenant with his fore-
fathers. Moses died and was buried "in a valley in the land of
Moab, over against Beth-peor" (Deut. 34:6).

The Damming of the Jordan

The Biblical text says that when the feet of the priests who
bore the ark touched the brink of the Jordan the
waters rose up in a heap, not where the Israelites were
crossing but far off, at a place called Adam (Josh. 3:15-16).
This place still bears the Arabic equivalent ed-Damieh where
the verdant valley of Faria joins the Jordan Valley from the
west. A small tell located here marks a Late Bronze and Iron
Age town which guarded this important ford; roads lead up
the valleys to the east and west. The Bible identifies the small
town Adam by saying it was alongside Zarethan (Josh. 3:16).
The text does not call Zarethan a city, although the mother
city of this district did have that name. Most agree that the
city itself is Tell es-Saadiyeh.[32] At ed-Damieh the river flows
through steep limestone cliffs where erosion can cause an
occasional landslide which dams the river. As late as 1927 the
river was dammed for twenty-one hours here.[33] The Hebrew
text of Joshua 3:15-16 is difficult. The author feels the text
implies a secondary cause which stopped the waters near
Adam at a divinely appointed time. Others, however, feel the
text means that the waters became a congealed heap from
where the priests stepped in all the way to Adam. The
interpretation centers around a very obtuse use of the
Hebrew preposition *b*. The phrase *be'ādām* can mean "in" or
"at" or even "from" Adam, but it is unlikely that it means
"to" Adam.

The Israelites performed a dual task on this occasion,
according to the account in Joshua 4. In obedience to a

command of God they lifted twelve stones from the river bed near the place where the priests stood and set them up as a memorial in the camp on the western side (vv. 3-8). Similarly, Joshua built a monument in the river bed at the place where the priests stood. Such a double ceremony need not indicate that there were two versions of the story.[34]

The Israelites camped at Gilgal after they crossed the Jordan. Joshua 4:19 tells us it was on the east border of Jericho. As in the case of Zarethan, Jericho may have been the name of the entire oasis for which the walled city provided protection (Josh. 17:16, Jon. 3:3). We should look for Gilgal somewhere on the eastern fringe of the Jericho oasis. Slightly to the northeast of Tell es-Sultan is Khirbet el-Mefjir, where in 1963 D.C. Baramki excavated an elaborate Muslim palace of the Ummayid ruler Hisham (eighth century A.D.). J. Muilenburg explored the region in 1955 and would like to locate Joshua's Gilgal near Mefjir although most of his evidence is literary rather than archaeological.[35] If this is not the correct site, Gilgal has yet to be identified.

The Conquest of Jericho

Jericho had been destroyed at the end of the Middle Bronze Age (ca. 1580) by New Kingdom kings who drove out the Hyksos. Kenyon says: "When the material is analyzed in the light of present knowledge it becomes clear that there is a complete gap both on the Tell and in the tombs between 1580 B.C. and 1400 B.C."[36] During these years Palestine came firmly under the power of Egypt.

The Amarna Letters show that Palestine was made up of many different racial elements about 1400 B.C. City-state rulers with Canaanite, Babylonian and Hurrian (Horite) names were dependent on Egypt but, as we have seen, her control of Palestine, while real, was not as strong as in the preceding century under Thutmose III. The molesting 'Apiru and the general condition of political instability prepared the way for

An airview of the mound of ancient Jericho. Modern Jericho is in the background.

Israelite entry into the land. It is unlikely that Israel could have continued to escape Egyptian domination unless the political picture was such as appears in the Amarna letters. Egyptian control stiffened again around 1300, when Seti I set about to regain Asiatic domains for Egypt.

The excavation of Jericho by John Garstang was done in the thirties before pottery chronology was adequately understood for the Late Bronze period. As a result Garstang's interpretations were erroneous in some important points. Garstang mistook an Early Bronze Age wall to be the wall destroyed under Joshua. Two parallel walls, one six feet thick and the other twelve feet thick, he thought were part of a casemate wall of Joshua's time. There were signs of a great conflagration, thick ash between the walls and in the city (Josh. 6:24). Garstang also found scarabs of Amenhotep III (until 1385) in the nearby tombs,[37] which proves the city was inhabited during or after Amenhotep's time, but does not give a terminal date for its destruction. Miss Kenyon revealed that the two walls were not contemporaneous and that a Hyksos (until 1550) scarp covered both of them. The latest city wall extant on the tell, according to Kenyon, is Middle Bronze. The remains of a small building and Garstang's "Middle Building," which he placed in the Iron Age, are all Kenyon could identify as coming from the Late Bronze period on the tell.

Miss Kenyon maintains that some evidence for a Late Bronze destruction of Jericho exists but that it does not tell a coherent story.[38] The reason for this incoherence lies in the lack of sufficient evidence because of the erosion of the Late Bronze levels. The combination of violent winter rains and intense summer sun turns the soil to fine dust and leads to extreme erosion. The tombs away from the tell prove conclusively that the city was occupied in the Late Bronze period and that it was during the Late Bronze times that the biggest pottery change occurred; the culture between Late Bronze I and II showed marked deterioration. Such deterioration might mark a change in material sophistication brought about by the Hebrew conquest.[39] Kenyon would put the destruc-

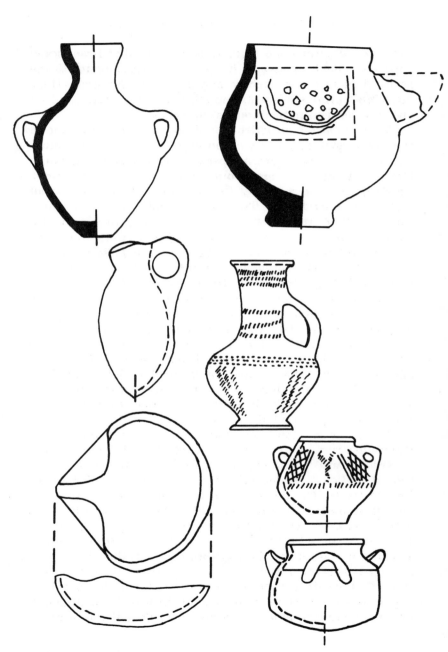

LATE BRONZE AGE POTTERY FROM JERICHO

tion of Jericho under Joshua sometime in the fourteenth century, which would fit neither the late date (thirteenth century) nor the very early date in the fifteenth century. [40] Kenyon's preference is about 1325 for the fall of the city, which she conjectures was quite small at the time. One wonders if this conjecture is not too precise in the light of her own statement that "the time-scale by which we at present attempt to fix chronology is by no means exact for this period of the Late Bronze Age."[41]   Hence we have no dramatic evidence of crumbled walls such as Garstang claimed; nevertheless, the available evidence does tend to support a destruction of the site and subsequent abandonment sometime in the Late Bronze Age.

Kenyon asserts in her article in *Archaeology and Old Testament Study*[42] that it is impossible to date the destruction of Jericho in the thirteenth century as W. F. Albright and others have suggested. If there was a thirteenth century Exodus, then the archaeological evidence for the destruction of Jericho in the Late Bronze Age does not correspond to it. M. Noth has concluded that the Biblical story is etiological, that is, fabricated to explain historical circumstances. It could just be possible that an earlier date for the Exodus might be the correct approach. One of the major arguments for the thirteenth century date has been Nelson Glueck's surface sherd evidence that Transjordan was not occupied until that time.[43]   But his evidence from surface sherd studies appears to be less valid than was once thought.[44]   The destruction of other cities such as Hazor, Debir, and Lachish in the thirteenth century remains the only major evidence for a late Exodus and conquest. Even in these cities there are no major pottery changes until about 1100 B.C., which is too late for the arrival of Israel.[45]

The Danites Take Laish

Judges 18 tells how the tribe of Dan sought out a new home in the territory around the sources of the Jordan. They took the city of Laish (Leshem) where the people "dwelt in security after the manner of the Sidonians" (18:7). The area was attached to the Phoenician coastal area, as noted in Numbers 13:29, "the Canaanites dwell by the sea and along the Jordan." Judges 18:7, 28 makes it clear that the people of Laish were sufficiently removed from their own people that the Danites had no difficulty in taking the city. They renamed it Dan. Hazor, which could have helped, and the other kings mentioned in Joshua 11, whom Joshua defeated at the waters of Merom (vv. 5-7), were no longer available. Hazor was temporarily in Israelite hands.

A monumental city gate of Tell Dan came to light in 1968. The excavation was carried on by A. Biran who believes this gate (about 87 by 55 feet), the great city wall, and a paved street connected with it were all the work of Jeroboam I, who set up a golden calf in Dan (I Kings 12:28, 29). Jeroboam made it an administrative center and fortress to withstand foreign armies. The gate was destroyed in the first half of the ninth century, probably by Benhadad of Damascus. Impressive earlier fortifications date to the Middle Bronze Age. The city at this earlier period was called Laish both in the Bible and in Egyptian Execration Texts. The Mari Texts from middle Mesopotamia mention Laish as a city which exported wine. The city was destroyed by fire at the end of the seventeenth century and of course was conquered by the Danites early in the eleventh century. The Danites used the earlier fortifications until Jeroboam I rebuilt the city. A building of the sixth century was excavated, which confirms Jeremiah's references to the city in Jeremiah 4:15 and 8:16.[46]

Hazor and the Hebrews

Another extensive excavation which tells us about Middle Bronze and Late Bronze Jordan Valley is the site of Hazor, which overlooks the Huleh Valley from the southwest. The city had a strategic location on a main junction into Palestine from the north and east, guarding the natural place for crossing the Jordan at the present Bridge of the Daughters

Relics of the temple at Hazor on display at Haifa Museum.

of Jacob. Excavations have been carried on at Tell el-Qedah (Hazor) by Y. Yadin under the sponsorship of the Israel Exploration Fund. The site is divided into two parts: the tell on which the Hebrew city was built, and a wide area of raised ground with a great earthen fortification around it similar to the ramparts the Hyksos perfected. Yadin located one city on top of another, going back to the mid-third millennium. In Middle Bronze II (ca. 1850) an upsurge in building took place in the so-called lower city. A prize find was a twenty-five foot wide city wall made of bricks on a stone foundation and covered with plaster. This series of Canaanite cities covering a wide area confirms the greatness of Hazor. Literary knowledge of Hazor goes back to its mention in the Egyptian Execration Texts[47] of the nineteenth century B.C. It is the only Palestinean city mentioned in the Mesopotamian Mari letters of ca. 1700 B.C.[48] Hazor was of sufficient importance to get into the annals of the New Kingdom pharaohs Thutmose III, Amenhotep II, and Seti I,[49] and in the Amarna correspondence between Egyptian kings and their Asiatic vassals. The Amarna Letters tell of a rivalry between Hazor and Tyre. In an Egyptian document from the thirteenth century, called Papyrus Anastasi I, the writer, a royal official, questions his correspondent about the route to Hazor and the stream that is near it, meaning obviously the Jordan.[50]

We are not surprised then to find in Joshua 11:10, ". . . for Hazor beforetime was the head of all those kingdoms." Yadin claims there is evidence of Joshua's burning of Hazor (Josh. 11:13) in the thirteenth century. He also mentions a great conflagration of the elaborate Late Bronze gate of the lower city which preceded the thirteenth century destruction. There were 30 acres in the upper city and 175 acres in the lower enclosure. Such a complex could not be easily destroyed. In four seasons the excavators uncovered only 1/400 of the site. The author is familiar with Sumerian date formulae which speak of cities being destroyed for the ninth time, which means that each "destruction" was only a token affair.[51] That Joshua's original conquests were not final is evident from Judges 4:2 which says Israel's control of the land came gradually.

Among the coalition of kings who came to Israel according to Joshua 11 were those living in the valley (Arabah) south of Chinnereth on the southern shore of the Lake of Galilee. These were undoubtedly from Beth-shan and her neighboring towns. Joshua surprised this northern coalition at the waters of Merom; that is, the springs which flow by the town of Meiron, west of Safed. In this rugged country the many Canaanite chariots (11:4) could not be used strategically. Joshua chased some of the enemy into the valley of Mizpeh

(11:8). Y. Aharoni takes this to be the valley between Metulla and Marj-ayoun. Joshua's destruction of Hazor, however, must have been ephemeral because a later Jabin, king of Hazor, supplied chariots to fight Israel in the valley of Esdraelon (Judg. 4 and 5). The Biblical picture is also complete with the statement that the Israelites took the mountain country but could not take the valley plains where the Canaanites made strategic use of their chariots of iron (Judg. 1:19). Deborah's song suggests that God used a divinely timed storm to make the valley of Esdraelon a marsh, so bogging the chariots of Hazor's King Jabin that they became a liability rather than an asset (Judg. 5:19-22). So in this case Israel had a victory in a valley plain rather than in the hill country.

Late Bronze Age Hazor had an estimated population of about forty thousand. The upper city's palace showed the work of master masons with a plastered cistern eighty to ninety feet long, a new invention for holding emergency water. Yadin labeled one of the temples in the lower city the orthostat temple because of straight slabs of basalt forming a dado around a large main hall. There were three wings, a porch, main hall, and holy of holies broadly resembling Solomon's temple in Jerusalem. This was built in the Late Bronze Age and was destroyed at the end of Late Bronze II (second half of the thirteenth century). In it was found parts of a basalt statue of a god standing on a bull with the emblem of the god Hadad (the crossed sun-disk) carved on it. The Canaanite equivalent of Hadad was Baal. In the fourteenth century version of this same temple the excavators found an orthostat of a crouching lion (5'10" long), one of a pair guarding the entrance to the temple. Sculpture of this type comes from Syria and is similar to a fourteenth century lion orthostat from Beth-shan.

An earlier temple dating from the fifteenth century, was simpler but featured a large monumental gateway. In this temple a clay model of an animal's liver was found, inscribed with omens in cuneiform writing, for use by the temple diviners. Yadin notes that the sun-god is the god of liver-diviners so the temple must have been associated in some way with sun worship. A stela was also found depicting worshipful hands held up toward a crescent moon with a "sun" disc within, similar to the symbol used in Hittite hieroglyphics to signify the Mesopotamian moon god Sin. [52] All this reminds us of Moses's severe warnings to the Israelites concerning Canaanite divination and worship of the heavenly bodies (Deut. 4:19; 17:3; 18:9-14). A third temple in the lower city of Hazor went back to Hyksos times (1700).

The upper city of Hazor (the Acropolis) is where the Canaanite kings built their palaces. This is the part of the city the Israelites, beginning with Solomon, rebuilt. But there were two phases of Israelite occupation before Solomon rebuilt the city. The later phase was a small settlement without a city wall which, Yadin says, had an idolatrous Israelite cult-place including incense stands and a figurine of a war god. Yadin ties this to the period of the judges which describes such open idolatry in Israel (Judg. 18). The earlier Israelite settlement was no more than a seminomadic encampment on the ruins of the Canaanite city. Yadin dates it to the mid-twelfth century.

Solomon rebuilt Hazor with a great gate and strong casemate walls, and it became a fortress guarding Israel's northern frontier. In Ahab's time the city received some fine architecture as may be judged from two proto-Ionic capitals such as were found at Megiddo and in Samaria, but in Hazor a dressed column on which one of the capitals rested was also found. The city continued until 732, when the invading Assyrian army of Tiglath-pileser destroyed it.

The Valley Around Beth-shan
in the Late Bronze and Iron Periods

The strategic fortress of Beth-shan at the junction of the Esdraelon valley, guarded this entrance into the hills of Palestine. Scarabs at Beth-shan point to Egyptian domination there beginning with Thutmose III (ca. 1470). Beth-shan was captured by Thutmose III after his famous battle at Megiddo

Mekal Stele, Late Bronze Age Beth-shan. Mekal, on the left, is receiving a lotus from Amen-em-apt, builder of the temple.

(1468) which remained an Egyptian garrison during the Amarna Age and into the Ramesside Period (ca. 1300). Evidence of the conquest of this area is found in a stela fragment of Thutmose III (or Amenhotep II) at Chinnereth (Tell el-Oreimeh) on the Sea of Galilee.[53] Another complete stela found at Beth-shan shows an Egyptian architect whose name was Amen-em-Opet worshiping the Canaanite deity Mekal, the Lord (Baal) of Beth-shan. The god is a typical

Excavations at Tell Beisan (Beth-shan).

Asiatic with pointed beard and conical headdress with horns and streamers. The stela reveals the eclectic nature of Egyptian religion for those who lived abroad at this time, for the architect addresses this Asiatic god in the regular terminology of an Egyptian mortuary prayer.[54]

Egyptian power even under Thutmose III was sometimes spotty. The hill country apparently did not interest the Egyptians. They entered the country on the *Via Maris* along the coast. The route is called "the way of the land of the Philistines" in Exodus 13:17. This route passed through the Carmel range into the plain of Esdraelon, thence eastward by Beth-shan to Damascus, or from Beth-shan by way of the Jordan Valley to the Hazor pass and on to the Phoenician coast and thence to Kadesh on the Orontes. After Thutmose III, Egyptian imperialism waned and Beth-shan with her Jordan Valley daughter towns remained in the hands of Canaanite chieftains. This made the children of Joseph complain later. "The hill country is not enough for us; and all the Canaanites that dwell in the valley have chariots of iron, both they who are of Beth-shan and her towns, and they who are of the valley of Jezreel" (Josh. 17:16).

This Biblical distinction between the culture of the valley and the hill country is believed to mark the two major cultural provinces of the Holy Land in the Middle and Late Bronze Ages.[55] The materially high culture of the Jordan Valley and the valley of Esdraelon had come from Phoenicia and spread through Syria into Palestine (Num. 13:29; Josh.

Top, left: This basalt panel from Late Bronze Age Beth-shan is a good example of Hittite-type workmanship.

Middle: A Canaanite man (right) and woman (left) are depicted on these jar fragments from Late Bronze Age Beth-shan.

Bottom right: Stela of goddess Antit (queen of heaven). The godess is depicted on the left. The figure on the right is a male singer of Nekht. From Beth-shan, Iron Age I.

Top, right, and bottom, left: Iron Age incense stands from the temple of Astarte in Beth-shan.

11:3). In the valley areas this high culture persisted. Both the Hyksos and later the Hebrews adapted to the preexistent cultural patterns. The Hyksos added materially, as in the case of improved city defenses, while the Hebrews of the Late Bronze Age had mainly a spiritual heritage to offer. From the time of Thutmose III, Egyptian political power was always a factor to be dealt with but it was stronger in the valleys and plains than in the hill country. So it was much easier for the Hebrew presence to be felt in the hill country of both Transjordan and Cisjordan.

Egyptian power around Beth-shan was reasserted by Seti I (ca. 1300), who left several inscribed stelae which tell how he went about setting the area in order. In the most important of these stelae Seti mentions four cities in the Jordan Valley near Beth-shan; they are in addition to Beth-shan itself: Rehob, Pahel, Yenoam and Hamath. The stela reads in part: (A messenger is speaking to his majesty Seti I):

> " 'The wretched foe who is in the town of Hamath is gathering to himself many people, while he is seizing the town of Beth-shan. Then there will be an alliance with them of Pahel. He does not permit the Prince of Rehob to go outside.' Thereupon his majesty sent the first army of Amon (named) 'Mighty of Bows,' to the town of Hamath, the first army of Re (named) 'Plentiful of Valor,' to the town of Beth-shan, and the first army of Seth (named) 'Strong of Bows,' to the town of Yanoam. When the space of a day had passed, they were overthrown to the glory of his majesty, the king of Upper and Lower Egypt . . . "[56]

Pahel is Pella (Khirbet Fahil), destined to become a city of the Roman Decapolis. It is located on the eastern edge of the valley in the foothills across from Beth-shan. The site yielded to limited excavation in 1963 and 1967 when Late Bronze Age tombs were discovered which are said to be the most extensive of this period from anywhere in Palestine and Transjordan.[57] The tell itself is 1300 feet long, 750 wide, and 100 feet high. A strong spring is connected with it. Like other early cities, it is mentioned first in the Egyptian Execration Texts (nineteenth century) by its old Semitic name, Pihilum. The city flourished in the Middle and Late Bronze Ages, especially in

Top portion of stela of Seti I, dated 1313 B.C., found in Beth-shan. Seti, left, is offering "wings of Behudet" to his god Ra-Harmachis. The rest of the stela records a battle in which invaders from beyond the Jordan were repulsed by Seti's troops.

the fourteenth and thirteenth centuries. The city plays no part in the Biblical record, perhaps because it was a non-Hebrew city in the periods when it flourished most. This was certainly true in Hellenistic and New Testament times (pp. 124, 125).

Rehob and Hamath are probably at Tell el-Sarem, three miles south of Beth-shan, and Tell Hammeh, ten miles south of Beth-shan.[58] Garstang identified Yenoam with Tell Abeidiyah, which is just south of the southern tip of the Sea of Galilee on the west bank of the Jordan. Albright located Yenoam at modern Tell en-Naameh north of Lake Huleh.[59] It has suggested that Seti's real opposition was from the Hittites. He therefore put a roadblock at Yenoam to cut off supplies from the north so he could deal effectively with the rebellion around Beth-shan.[60] Beth-shan and its neighboring cities were guardians of numerous important fords of the northern part of the valley. But Beth-shan, as mentioned, was the mother fortress because it was the most strategically located, connecting the cities of Gilead and Damascus with the cities of the plain of Esdraelon, and for that matter all of the hill country.

The aforementioned document from the thirteenth century, Papyrus Anastasi I, also refers to Beth-shan and Rehob. Hori, the learned Egyptian writer of the papyrus, chides his correspondent:

> Pray teach me about the appearance of Qiyen, let me know Rehob, explain Beth-shan and Tirqa-El. The stream of Jordan, how is it crossed? Let me know the way to pass Megiddo, which is above it.[61]

In still another document, a Beth-shan stela, number 885 in the Rockefeller Palestine Museum, Seti I tells of military action in the Jordan Valley. A messenger came to tell the king: "The Apiru of Mount Yarmuta . . . have arisen in attack upon the Asiatics of Rehem."[62] This text proceeds to say that his majesty, Seti, put down the rebellion with his infantry and numerous chariots. The city Yarmuth, which must have received or given its name to the river of that name, is mentioned in Joshua 21:29. Albright says it was near Belvoir (Kokab el-Hawa), twelve miles north of Beth-shan in the valley.[63]

While Seti was successful in pushing the Egyptian frontier as far as Kadesh on the Orontes, where he defeated the Hittites and erected a victory stela, his two strongest successors, Ramses II (ca. 1250) and Ramses III (ca. 1170), had to fall back to such fortresses as Beth-shan. Ramses II solved his problems with the Hittites by a treaty[64] but both Ramses III and the Hittites were vigorously attacked by hordes of Sea

Stela of Ramses II found at Beth-shan. This stela was found along with a stela of Seti I and a statue of Ramses III in the ruins of an Egyptian fortress built by Seti I.

People, among whom were the Philistines and their cousins. The attack came not only by sea but also by land,[65] making Galilee and the valley around Beth-shan the frontier. Throughout his reign Ramses III continued to hold his Asiatic territory in Palestine, as his statue found at Beth-shan bears out. He also tells us of building a temple for Amon in Palestine and of owning nine towns there which paid him regular tribute.[66] Ramses III's only statement of a campaign against Semitic people is a reference to the people of Seir, whom he calls bedouin. These were probably the Edomites south of the Dead Sea.[67] But Egypt's glory was now past, for Ramses III's successor withdrew to the Nile Valley and the Jordan Valley was left open to invaders.[68]

The Jordan Valley and the Hebrew Judges and Kings

The valley continued to play a significant role during the days of the judges and kings. The careers of Ehud and Gideon were partially shaped by events which took place in the valley. The feud between Gileadites and the Ephraimites in the time of Jephthah (Judg. 11, 12) came to a head at the fords of the Jordan. In each of these three stories the fords of the Jordan were important.

In the days of Ehud an alliance of Moabites, Ammonites, and Amalekites crossed the Jordan and took "the city of palms" (Judg. 3:13), which at this time was probably a settlement in the Jericho oasis. The city that Joshua had destroyed was still in ruins and under a curse (Josh. 6:26). II Chronicles 28:15 identifies a "city of palms" in the days of Ahaz with Jericho, which could by that time have been the old Tell es-Sultan rebuilt by Hiel, the Bethelite (I Kings 16:34). Archaeology offers no evidence for this rebuilding. Iron Age remains at Tell es-Sultan are slight and date from the seventh century, which is after the building of the city by Hiel. In keeping with Joshua's curse on Jericho (Josh. 6:26) the Bible records a gap of 450 years while due to the severe erosion archaeology shows a gap of about 650 years.[69]

After Israel had paid tribute to Eglon, the king of Moab, for eighteen years, an Israelite hero managed to assassinate the fat Moabite monarch (Judg. 3:15-23). During the escapade a place called "the sculptured stones" near Gilgal is mentioned (Judg. 3:19). After performing his bloody deed Ehud escaped by passing again "the sculptured stones" and proceeded on to Seirah, an unknown place in the eastern mountains of Ephraim (Judg. 3:26). We are not told where Ehud met Eglon but it seems reasonable to assume that it was in the Jordan Valley, perhaps at the Jericho oasis. The "cool roof chamber" (v. 20) sounds like a place well suited to the Jordan Valley. Gilgal and the sculptured stones would have been to the north of the oasis if Ehud passed them again in escaping to the mountains of Ephraim. But Joshua 4:19 locates Gilgal on the east border of Jericho. In Hebrew there would not be a clear-cut distinction between east and northeast. We have already mentioned that Gilgal was in the vicinity of the Ummayid palace at Mefjir, which is northeast of Old Testament Jericho. Ehud gathered an army and returned to the valley to seize the nearby fords of the Jordan, trapping the Moabites who remained on the western side. Today similar fords exist in the area, such as Makhadat Hajla (cf. Beth-hoglah, Josh. 15:6; 18:19, 21) and Al Maghtas. The account states that the Moabites were driven from the valley west of the Jordan and implies that they had gained control of the area north of the Arnon which had been taken from the Amorites and allotted to the tribe of Reuben.

The Gideon episode begins at the waters of Harod which flow by Beth-shan into the Jordan Valley. The Midianites fled from the valley of Jezreel (Judg. 7:1) to the Jordan Valley as far as Beth-shittah in the direction of Zarethan, as far as the border of Abel-meholah, in the direction of Tabbath (Judg. 7:22).[70] Both Abel-meholah and Beth-shittah were near fords of the Jordan. So Gideon called on the Ephraimites to join him in the Jordan Valley in order to capture the fords. In Judges 7:24 Gideon says, "Seize the waters from them, even the Jordan, as far as Beth-barah." The Madaba Mosaic Map shows a Beth-abara (ford town) guarding a major crossing not far from Jericho (p. 149). One is tempted to tie this Beth-barah with Beth-arabah of Joshua 15:6, even though it involves the transposing of two Hebrew letters. Judah's boundary started at the mouth[71] of the Jordan northward to Beth-hoglah,[72] then passed on north to Beth-arabah (Beth-abara?). Gideon, then, may have called for the seizing of all the fords of the Jordan south to the Dead Sea.

In Judges 8:4-6 Gideon himself, in pursuit of the Midianite

princes, passed over Jordan in the region of Succoth,[73] now believed to be at or near Tell Deir Alla. Nearby there are now four fords.[74] Succoth was not far from Zarethan (I Kings 7:46), and as mentioned above it is probable that Zarethan was the name of a whole district, for it was a big city like Beth-shan. I Kings 4:12, which gives the fifth district of Solomon's kingdom, names several sub-districts including "all Beth-shan which is beside Zarethan below Jezreel, from Beth-shan to Abel-meholah." Abel-meholah must be somewhere in the Zarethan district, not necessarily immediately adjacent to Deir Alla (Succoth?) but not far away. Since Elisha, who came from Abel-meholah, was plowing when Elijah found him (I Kings 19:15-21), the site is likely to be found on the east side of the *Ghor*, where farming would be prevalent. E. G. Kraeling suggests Tell el-Meqbereh, which is near the Jordan's rich bottom lands.[75]

The fords of the Jordan became important again in the

After a season of excavation at Deir Alla.

story of the feud between Jephthah's Gileadites and the proud Ephraimites, who were angry because Jephthah did not let them share in his victory over Ammon (Judg. 12:1). The Gileadites seized the fords of the Jordan and determined with a test of their dialect the tribal connections of those who wanted to cross. They knew the Ephraimites could not pronounce the *sh* in the word *Shibboleth* but invariably said *Sibboleth*. Such a dialectal difference shows again the importance of the Rift Valley as a cultural barrier. There are indications that Jephthah lived in the Jordan Valley, at Zaphon. The Septuagint text in Joshua 12:7 says that he was buried "in his city, Zaphon."

Crossing the fords of the Jordan was a way to escape from a molesting enemy. According to I Samuel 13:6-7, the Philistines forced the Israelites to hide in caves, rocks, tombs, and cisterns, but many crossed the fords of the Jordan to the land of Gad and Gilead for safety. In I Samuel 13 Saul with his little army of six hundred at Gilgal was probably assisting people to escape by securing the fords and waiting for the right moment to return to the hill country to fight. Later King Saul's struggle with the Philistines ended in his death in a battle on Mount Gilboa. Saul's armor was taken to the temple of Ashtaroth in Beth-shan (I Sam. 31:10). The extensive excavations at Beth-shan uncovered several eleventh century Canaanite temples.[76] Although the Philistines had extended political control over Beth-shan in the eleventh century, the absence of Philistine pottery in the time of Saul may indicate that the Philistines were only military overlords, and that the city never became a Philistine cultural center.[77] Clay anthropoid coffins of the type used by the Philistines have been found in the Iron I cemetery.[78] Effective Egyptian control of the city ended with the passing of Ramses III (1167), although some feel that the Philistines continued in control of the city as Egyptian mercenaries.[79] Israel had never taken Beth-shan even when Egyptian influence was weak (Josh. 17:11, 16; Judg. 1:27). Upon hearing of Saul's death the people who lived in and along the Jordan Valley[80]

Anthropoid coffin of the type found at Beth-shan.

again fled, leaving their cities, which the Philistines promptly occupied (I Sam. 31:7). Such a brief occupation shortly before David's conquests left little or no lasting Philistine impression.

Jabesh-gilead on the other side of the Jordan went unmolested. Just after Saul was anointed he saved Jabesh from

humiliation at the hands of Nahash the Ammonite (I Sam.
11). In loving response the elders of Jabesh made a nocturnal
visit to Philistine-controlled Beth-shan to recover and bury
the king's body, which was disgracefully attached to a wall (I
Sam. 31:13). Tell Maqlub, a site near the Wadi Yabis
(Jabesh), may be Jabesh-gilead. Glueck prefers to locate it in
the Jordan Valley at the dual sites of Tell Meqbereh and Tell
Abu Kharaz. He feels Maqlub is too far away for the Jabesh-
ites to have heard of the death of Saul, walked to Beth-shan,
and returned with the bodies of Saul and his sons in one
night.[81] This writer prefers Maqlub simply because it is more
likely to be considered a part of Gilead and because the text
of I Samuel 31:11 does not say that they heard the news of
Saul's death the same day. In addition, Maqlub is only six
miles from the Ghor and another six miles brings one to
Beth-shan.

David and the Jordan Valley

David's early career brought him into intimate contact
with the Philistines in their southern coastal territory around
the Philistine pentapolis.[82] In I Samuel 23:24-28 David and
his men were hiding in the wilderness of Maon, an especially
barren and rugged part of the Judean wilderness along the
southern half of the Dead Sea. Saul hotly pursued them,
chasing David's band around one of the mountains. The
pursuit was abruptly halted when Saul responded to an
impending Philistine threat. David then went to rest in the
strongholds of En-gedi. The fresh water springs and torturous
precipices made En-gedi an excellent retreat. Such a name as
"the Wild-Goats Rocks" (I Sam. 24:2) gives some idea of the
nature of this area, where slopes rise unbroken for hundreds
of feet. Saul searched for David in the wilderness around
En-gedi, his men climbed over the rocks usually inhabited
only by the wild goats. To this day travelers are amazed at
the wild goats near the "Spring of the Kid" (En-gedi) as these
animals incredibly stick like glue to steep slopes (Hab. 3:19).

The cliffs of the Jordan Valley at Engedi.

The poet in Song of Solomon likens his beloved to "a cluster of henna blossoms from the vineyards of En-gedi" (Song of Sol. 1:14). These vineyards must have been on the valley floor and must have been irrigated from the springs, as is the case today in the nearby kibbutz.

Many years later David again sought relief from his pursuers by entering the Jordan Valley. This time it was to reach the fords of Jordan while in flight from Absalom (II Sam. 17:22). His destination was Mahanaim, a place somewhere near the junction of the Jabbok and the Jordan. Mahanaim, meaning "Two Camps," had received its Hebrew name when Jacob divided his household at the Jabbok before meeting Esau (Gen. 32). Later the town of Mahaniam, then a principal city, became the capital of Ishbosheth, Saul's son and successor. At the invitation of the Gileadites David used the town as a stronghold during his son Absalom's rebellion.

David maintained a line of communication across the Jordan Valley which ended in the person of Hushai, his secret agent in Jerusalem. Mahanaim is generally thought to be Tell el-Hajjaj, a sizable site just south of the river Jabbok or it may be the more western Tell edh-Dhahab. An interesting episode involving the Jordan Valley developed at Mahanaim following the slaying of Absalom in II Samuel 18:19-33. Ahimaaz, the son of Zadok the priest, wanted to run and be the first to tell David of Absalom's death, but Joab, knowing of David's emotional attachment to Absalom, sent instead a Cushite mercenary. Later Ahimaaz was also allowed to go and he went "by the way of the plain" (v. 23), that is, along the floor of the Jordan Valley. Because the Cushite ran up and down the hilly and wooded (?) terrain of Gilead, Ahimaaz got there first but then lost his nerve and waited for the Cushite to arrive and tell David (vv. 29-32).

The ever resourceful David carefully mended his fences with the leaders of Judah (II Sam. 19:11-15) and the men of Judah came down to meet him in the Jordan Valley at Gilgal and conducted the king over the Jordan (v. 15). A ferryboat went over to carry the king's household across the river (v. 18). The Israelites from the north also arrived at Gilgal and from there we hear a rumble of distrust from the northerners, who complained that the men of Judah had stolen the king away from them (vv. 41-43). Sheba, a Benjamite, sought to take advantage of this discontent by calling for outright secession of the northern tribes. Joab pursued Sheba to a city on the slopes of Mount Hermon near the stream Bareighit, one of the sources of the Jordan. That city was Abel-beth-maacah (Tell Abil) overlooking the Huleh Valley (II Sam. 20:15). The wisdom of an unnamed woman saved the city from destruction. She called the city "a mother in Israel" (v. 19), meaning a very old and historic place known as a center of ancient culture and wisdom (v. 18). Then she persuaded the elders to throw the head of the rebel Sheba over the city wall and bloody Joab turned away satisfied. The site of this famous city (Tell Abil) near the sources of the Jordan awaits excavation.

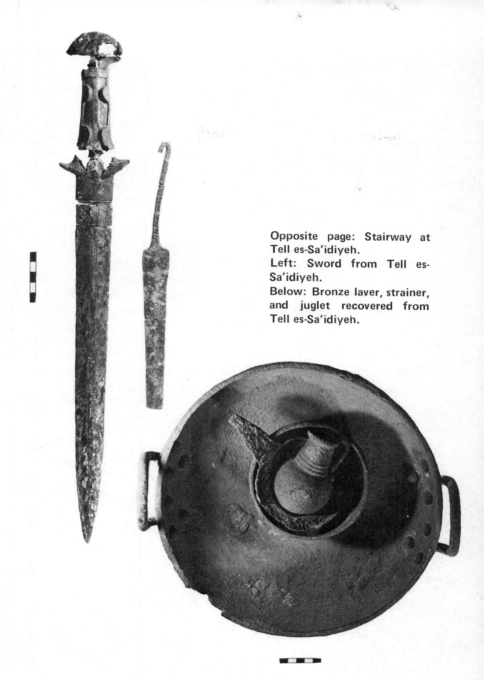

Opposite page: Stairway at Tell es-Sa'idiyeh.
Left: Sword from Tell es-Sa'idiyeh.
Below: Bronze laver, strainer, and juglet recovered from Tell es-Sa'idiyeh.

Solomon and the Jordan Valley

Wadi Faria from the west and the Jabbok from the east join the Jordan near the ford called ed-Damieh. Nelson Glueck lists seven reasons for locating Zarethan of Joshua 3:16 at Tell es-Saadiyeh, twelve miles north of ed-Damieh. [83] While no one doubts the location of Adam (Josh. 3:16) at Damieh, we do not have final proof that Saadiyeh is Zarethan. Glueck makes a strong case for this location from surface pottery, the size of the mound, and its position. Saadiyeh is only one mile from the edge of the Zor on Wadi Kufrinji. No other site is big enough to be as well known as the Bible implies and only this site guards so well the approaches from both the west and the rich valley to the east.

The tell covers twenty acres and stands about one hundred feet above the arable valley floor, which is now plentifully irrigated by the canal system which brings water from as far away as the Yarmuk. Excavation began here in February 1964 under J. B. Pritchard, sponsored by the Museum of the University of Pennsylvania. Four seasons have been completed. Almost immediately on top of the tell stands an eighth century B.C. housing area having many houses of a uniform size and style all sharing a common back wall. Such architecture proves there was prearranged communal planning and therefore a highly organized community. A stairway was part of a underground water system like those at Megiddo and Jerusalem. Also a Late Bronze-Early Iron Age cemetery contained interesting tombs, one of a "queen" in a brick-lined tomb had a large quantity of personal articles such as beads, toggle pins, etc. made of gold, carnelian, and electrum. An ivory box with sliding lid was decorated with rosettes and a bull's head. An ivory spoon of Egyptian design was also found. A considerable number of bronze items, among them a Cypriote tripod, a large caldron, a bronze lamp, drinking bowls, and strainers, reminded Pritchard of I Kings 7:45-46: "And the pots, and the shovels, and the basins; and all these vessels, which Hiram made for king Solomon for the house of the Lord, were of bright brass. In the plain of Jordan did the king cast them, in the clay ground between Succoth and Zarethan."[84] But it should be remembered that these bronzes are from a much earlier time than Solomon, for the tombs date from the thirteenth and fourteenth centuries. Surface investigations around this area did reveal slag remains of the Solomonic metal industry. The clay of the valley floor provided excellent molds for casting the metal objects such as the laver[85] and other utensils for the temple.

Solomon also had a complete mining industry in the Arabah, where small quantities of copper had been mined and smelted as early as Chalcolithic times. Solomon revived and expanded the industry in a number of places in the Rift Valley. One of these was about fifteen miles north of Elat (Elath) in the valley of Timnah where three arms of this wadi extend from the high country to the west. This is one of the earliest evidences of a complete copper industry at one place. Today many outcroppings of blue-green copper silicate can be seen in the nubian sandstone but this ore has only about 1.5 percent copper which could not be extracted by the ancients.[86] Studies have been made in this area by a British and Israeli team with reports in *The Palestine Exploration Quarterly*[87] which show that the ancients worked shallow mines of rich copper sulfide ore (40 to 50 percent copper) and also dug at the roots of petrified trees which were heavy in minerals like iron oxide used in the smelting process. Stone implements for mining and crushing ore have been dated to the ninth and tenth centuries by sherd evidence. Slag at nearby camps shows considerable smelting activity not far from the mines. Smelting was accomplished by the open pit method. There were no stone furnaces or even clay crucibles in the Timnah industry.

Another Solomonic mining site is at Wadi Amram, which also empties from the west into the Arabah five miles north of the Gulf. Here the copper industry was enhanced by a water system for channeling rain into cisterns. Both sites were well planned to keep open the lines of communication to insure supply and to move out the product. This required a defense system, which in turn necessitated a well-organized central government. Even in the days of Solomon the Edomites

harrassed poorly populated areas like the Arabah, so Solomon had set up a line of fortresses in the Arabah. They were
small but very strong and they guarded the water sources and
the crossroads. Careful examination of these sites has con-
firmed the presence of casemate walls typical of Solomonic
times. Tell el-Kheleifeh, just yards from the waters of the
gulf, was a fortified caravanserai and storehouse granary
connected with the port at Elath (Ezion-geber). A limited
amount of refining was also evident here.[88]   In the mining
camps there was no evidence of forced labor, prisons, walls,
or places to keep slaves. It seems the work was done season-
ally when the weather was not so hot. The moderate amount
of slag found makes it very clear that Solomon worked these
mines for only a few years. According to Rothenberg, Solomon probably shipped little of the copper out of the port
city of Ezion-geber. It was more likely used to supplement
the stores of copper that David had already amassed before
Solomon began building the temple.[89]   And there is no evidence of any violent destruction at these sites; they were
simply abandoned.

Although there was a Middle Bronze copper industry in
the Arabah, the first really consolidated industry came in the
time of Solomon. Then in Nabatean times (ca. 200 B.C. to
200 A.D.) considerable mining was carried on, as also in
Roman-Byzantine times. It seems that all along the Arabah
sufficient water was available to support small smelting sites.
Slag piles reveal small scale primitive smelters during all
periods. People made copper on a kind of home industry
scale. There is no copper ore to be found anywhere on the
west side of the Arabah north of the Wadi Timnah. The ore
for the smelters at Ein Zureib, one of the centers for the
Nabatean and Byzantine-Roman mining industry, was
brought from the eastern hills near Feinan (Punon), a copper
mining center from the Bronze Age on (pp. 11, 24, 45).

The method of smelting copper was much the same for all
periods. Studies of this method have been made at Wadies
Timnah and Amram. The ore was first crushed with stone
hammers, resulting in a mixture of ore and silicate. The

crushed stone was carefully hand picked to remove the ore, then the ore was crushed again and hand picked until it was quite fine. The final dressing was done by placing this hand-picked ore in shallow dishes cut into areas of flat limestone. Here the ore was crushed again into finer and finer granules and the silica was winnowed away. The ore was then sent to workshops at the smelting sites, where it was ground into even finer powder and mixed with iron oxide and pulverized charcoal; if necessary, limestone was added. This mixture was made into a charge which was then placed in a charcoal-filled hearth, a hole in the earth about three-fourths of a meter across. Sufficient heat was obtained with bellows, at which point the copper would melt into little beads and drip into a cone-shaped hole in the bottom of the hearth. One charge after another was placed into the furnace until enough copper was melted out to fill the bottom cone. Then the fire was extinguished and the copper ingot removed. The ingots weighed about seven kilograms but were still quite impure. They were shipped to places like Ezion-geber, where further refining took place before the copper was ready to be cast or shipped. The Jordan Valley between Succoth and Zarethan must have been such a refinery for smelting and casting. Impure copper ingots were sent up from the Arabah and the iron was sent down from the iron mines in the hills of Gilead to be refined.

The name Succoth (Tell Deir Alla?) was popularly derived from the word for the "booths" made for Jacob's animals (Gen. 33:16-17). Here the city's elders refused to feed the faint men of Gideon when they returned with camel ornaments as trophies (Judg. 8:15-21) instead of the severed hands of their enemies (see above). The imposing mound of Deir Alla, excavated by H. J. Franken between 1960 and 1964, will require more work before definite identification can be made.[90] Franken discovered a number of sanctuaries of the Late Bronze period but no defensive walls. Three clay tablets in a yet unknown script were also discovered. They seem to be related to the Mycenaean ware found there. Franken feels the tell might be the Gilgal of I Samuel 13:15

Early Iron Age vase from Deir Alla with "Sea People" (Philistine) decorations.

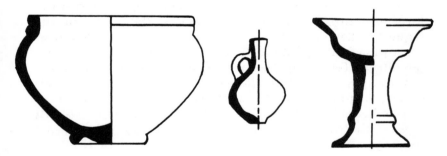

Other Early Iron Pottery from Deir Alla.

rather than Succoth, but if so, Succoth must be a tell nearby. Tell el-Ekhsas, one and a half miles west of Alla, means "Mound of Booths," but most feel the name shifted, as was so often the case, from the larger mound at Alla to Ekhsas. Pottery associated with nearby furnaces and copper slag shows that the metal industry of I Kings 7:46 continued long after the time of Solomon.

Three miles north of Deir Alla is Wadi Rajib, on which is located Tell Qos, which Glueck identified with the Biblical Zaphon (Josh. 13:27). But Aharoni prefers Tell es-Saadiyeh to the northwest of Qos despite literary evidence pointing to Qos in the Jerusalem Talmud.[91] At any rate it seems clear that in Judges 12:1, we should read "Zaphon" for "northward" (RSV), making this old fortress Jephthah's headquarters in his war with the Ephraimites. The city had been a Canaanite stronghold, according to a short bit of correspondence to the Egyptian king, Amenhotep IV, which came from the Princess of Zapuna (Zapon), who called herself "Lady of the Lions."[92] That Zaphon was an old and well-known town may be assumed from Joshua 13:27, where it is used in a boundary passage.

Solomon divided his kingdom into twelve administrative districts for tax purposes (I Kings 4:7-19). In the seventh district the city of Mahanaim (v. 14) was the seat of authority over the old towns of the eastern Jordan Valley including Zaphon, Succoth, Beth-nimrah, and Beth-haram. Across the river the fifth district (v. 12) included the towns of the Jezreel Valley and the western Jordan Valley from Beth-shan to Abel-meholah (Tell Hilu?) and Jokmeam (Tell Mazar?) and Zarethan (Tell Umm Hamad?). Pharaoh Shishak, following his invasion of Palestine after Solomon's death, inscribed on the walls of his temple at Karnak the names of the Palestinian towns he sacked. He speaks of "the Valley" and includes in his list the towns of Adam, Succoth, Zaphon, Rehob, and Beth-shan.[93]

The Days of Elijah and Elisha

With textual backing, Glueck, following the lead of G. A. Smith, claims that Elijah's brook Cherith was an eastern arm of Wadi Yabis. Elijah, suggests Glueck, was not "the Tishbite," but "the Jabeshite," and he went eastward according to I Kings 17:3 to Cherith, not westward, as would have been the case if Cherith were the Wadi Qelt near Jericho as tradition suggests.[94]

As noted above, the writer tends to agree with E. G. Kraeling that Tell el-Meqbereh is a likely site for the home of Elisha at Abel-meholah (I Kings 19:16). The site is near the *Zor* and is apparently well watered, which fits the Biblical requirement that Elijah found Elisha behind twelve yoke of oxen (v. 19). Since his home was in the *Ghor*, the valley and the river had a considerable bearing on Elisha's ministry. Naaman's bath in the muddy Jordan (II Kings 5), purification of the waters of Jericho (II Kings 1:19-22),[95] and the incident of the floating axehead (II Kings 6:1-7) all stress Elisha's attachment to the valley. The exact location of the latter miracle is not given, although it took place probably in the *Zor*, where wood was available. Elisha's proteges, the sons of the prophets, went to the Jordan to cut trees and build a dormitory.

The Biblical text both in Kings and Chronicles seems to indicate that in the days of Jehoshaphat the Edomites were largely under Judah's control. In II Kings 3 the Edomites assisted Judah and Israel against Mesha, king of Moab. On this occasion the battle was to take place in Edomite country "by way of the wilderness of Edom" (II Kings 3:8). The armies of Judah and Edom made a circuitous march of seven days through the Arabah and were hard pressed for water. They turned to Elisha who was with them. Out of concern for Jehoshaphat, Elisha predicted that water would be provided and that God would use this very water to bring deliverance from the Moabites. Without wind or rain an unnamed wadi on the east of the Arabah was flooded with water (v. 16). The next morning the water came from the direction of Edom (v. 20) until the country was filled with water. Later the Moabites from a distance saw the sun shining on the unsuspected water and took it to be blood. Believing the three armies had fallen to feuding they opened themselves to disaster by approaching the camp of Israel as men prepared to gather spoil (vv. 23-24). In this area in the spring of 1963 a freak combination of storms brought floods of water through the wadies which penetrate the hills east of the Arabah. About thirty tourists were swept to their death while passing through the narrow gorge at Petra (Wadi Musa). The day following this disaster the author witnessed pools of water, even small lakes everywhere in the desert, and yet the wind and rain of the storm itself had occurred in far off, unseen places.[96]

On another occasion the Moabites and their allies, the Ammonites and people of Mount Seir, penetrated across the Arabah to the western side of the Dead Sea (II Chron. 20) and Jehoshaphat took his army to meet them. The people of Mount Seir were probably not Edomites but Meunites (cf. Maan east of Petra), that is, Arab predecessors of the Nabateans (pp. 111-115). It appeared the battle would join at Hazazontamar (En-gedi)[97] but Judah did not have to fight because the Ammonites and Moabites fell to feuding with the people of Seir and they destroyed each other in the Jordan Valley at the ascent of Ziz, at the end of the valley (Wadi Ghar?) east of the wilderness of Jeruel (II Chron. 20:16). Perhaps verse 22 is telling us that latent distrust was stirred up by a strategic ambush of men in Meunite garb. Jehoshaphat and

Broken vase from Ezion-geber, Iron II painted and burnished slip and the seal impression from the ring of Jotham (the king?).

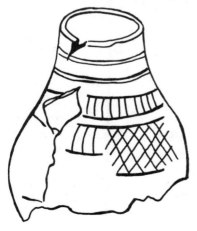

his Judean army came out through the wilderness of Tekoa to a "lookout point" (v. 24) in the wilderness and from here they viewed the devastation of their enemies. They descended and took spoil for three days before returning to the hill country for a thanksgiving service in the valley of Beracah (Blessing), a depression in the Judean hill country halfway between Hebron and Bethlehem.

David had conquered the Edomites and established control over Elath (Ezion-geber) on the Gulf of Aqabah. Solomon used Phoenician help in building an ocean fleet at Ezion-geber to trade for such prized commodities as the gold of Ophir (I Kings 9:26-28). Following Solomon the Hebrews had a continual contest with Edom for control of this area. When Judah was strong and Edom weak (I Kings 22:47) the Arabah became commercially important to the Hebrews. A road that led from the Gulf to Jerusalem[98] enabled Jehoshaphat to receive tribute from Arab kings (II Chron. 17:11). Continual discord between Judah and Edom centered around control of this trade route down the Arabah, for it meant possession of the copper mines, control of the seaport on the Gulf, and land trade into Arabia. Another trade route went from Sela (Petra) through the Arabah on south to Ezion-geber or west via Kurnub to Gaza and Ashkelon. Though more important in Nabatean times, the latter route carried slave traffic between Edom and Gaza during the Divided Kingdom (cf. Amos 2:6).[99] Jehoshaphat rebuilt the fleet at Ezion-geber, but it was destroyed before it put to sea, probably in the Edomite revolt of I Kings 22:47. The revolt continued into the reign of Jehoshaphat's son Joram. The Edomites successfully replaced the deputy governor Jehoshaphat had set over them (II Kings 8:20-22). For about a century they controlled the Arabah and Ezion-geber. According to II Kings 14:7 Amaziah killed ten thousand Edomites in the valley of Salt and captured Sela, which he renamed Joktheel (II Chron. 25:11, 12).[100] Uzziah completed the conquest of Edom by recovering Elath (II Chron. 26:1, 2: II Kings 14:22). Later under Ahaz Edom rebelled again and regained control of Elath (II Kings 16:6). From this point on Judah never again controlled Edom but the Edomites were too weak now to exploit the mines of the Arabah or to indulge in extensive sea and land trade. Nelson Glueck tells of stamped jars from Tell el-Kheleifeh bearing royal seals in archaic Hebrew-Edomite script which said: "Belonging to Qosanal, the servant of the king." These jars came from the sixth century B.C., final period of Edomite independence.[101]

The Jordan Valley in the Writings of Israel's Prophets and Poets

The writing prophets and poets of Israel used the features of the Jordan Valley in their literary figures. Such references are found in Jeremiah, Ezekiel, Zechariah, Job, and the Psalms. In several places Jeremiah draws on the characteristics of the *Zor* (thicket) to drive home a point. In Hebrew the *Zor* is called *ga'on* (jungle), which was confused by translators with a homonym which means "majesty" or "pride." In chapter 49:19 Jeremiah warns Edom that God "shall come up like a lion from the jungle (thicket) of the Jordan." Jeremiah 50:44 uses the same figure against Babylon. Because this tangle of willows, tamarisks, and cane made an excellent covert for wild animals such as lions in Biblical days, and even the wild boar until recently, it was considered a rather treacherous place. [102] Jeremiah warns the rebellious Israelites in chapter 12:5:

> If you have been in a foot-race and are
>   wearied,
>   how will you compete with horses?
> If you have fallen down in a safe land,
>   how will you make out in the jungle of the
>   Jordan?

In hyperbolic tones Zechariah in Chapter 11:3 envisions a day when the great cedars of Lebanon are ruined and the oaks of Bashan all are felled. All around is devastation and waste . . .

> "Listen to the wail of the shepherds,
>   for their glory is ruined!
> Listen to the roar of the lions,
>   for the jungle of the Jordan
>   is laid waste!"

Similarly when Ezekiel describes the boundaries of idealized Israel in chapter 47:18 he envisions the temple as a place from which sweet water issues and runs through the wilderness of Judah. The water runs down the Wadi en-Nar (Kidron) and out to the Dead Sea which in turn becomes sweet water so that fishermen can use nets along the shore from En-gedi to Ein-eglaim. The latter is thought by some to be an old name for Ein Feshkha near Qumran, although this would be the only place in the Bible where this spring is mentioned. We have noted the lushness of En-gedi referred to in the Song of Solomon 1:14 (p. 85). The Qumran people lived in part off the fish they caught in pools of Ein Feshkha. Ezekiel, of course, is speaking of sweetening the waters of the Dead Sea.

Borrowing a figure from the Jordan Valley, Zephaniah creates just the opposite impression in chapter 2:9, where he warns the Moabites that their land will be like the desolation of Sodom, "a land possessed by nettles and salt pits, and a waste forever." This is obviously a description of the aforementioned Sebkha, the salt flats south of the Dead Sea (p. 13).

There are only two passages in the Old Testament where the term Jordan (*Yardēn*) is used without the definite article. Both are poetry, where the article is sometimes omitted because of the archaizing tendency of the poetry. The first passage in Psalm 42:6 is a unique reference to "the land of Jordan" and a distinct reminder of the *Egyptian Topographical Lists*, [103] which mention Jordan as a territory. The psalmist says:

> My soul is sad within me!
> Therefore I remember you from the land of Jordan,
>   even from the Hermons and Mount Mizar.
> Deep is calling to deep
>   at the sound of your waterfalls.
> All your waves and billows have gone over me.

The Jordan country here may be the land of the three summits of Hermon, the sources of the Jordan. G. A. Smith in an excellent note observes that Khirbet Mezara and Wadi Zaura near Banias suggest an ancient "hill Mizar;" [104] the waves and the waterfalls of the psalm bring to mind the gushing water sources. This is only one interpretation of the psalm. How can water freshets be called waves and billows and why does he associate his sadness with the sources of the Jordan? M. Dahood answers by taking "the land of Jordan" as "the land of descent," a poetic name for the nether world. To do this he must slightly emend the Hebrew text. For example, *hermōnīm* he relates to *herem*, meaning "net." Psalm 18:6 and Job 5:5 show that Sheol was described as a place of nets and snares according to Dahood. Like Jonah in the fish descending into Sheol (Jon. 2:7) so the psalmist, at least metaphorically, has gone down to Sheol, "the land of Jordan." [105] The passage is difficult but the former interpretation fits the context better.

The other poetic reference to the Jordan where no article is used is Job 40:23. In the divine theophany Job hears a description of the mighty "behemoth," a primordial creation of God. The beast stands in the marshes shaded by lotus trees and is described with this couplet:

> Though the river oppresses him,
> he is not alarmed.
> He is confident,
> though the Jordan surges against his mouth.

Rather than the hippopotamus which existed in the Nile Delta, it is probably better to liken the "behemoth" to the water buffalo of the marsh-land of Lake Huleh. [106] Some feel the language here is mythological. "River" and "Jordan" are thought to be epithets of the river god. It was, however, a Hebrew innovation to demythologize such terminology.

This innovation is even clearer in the highly figurative description of the Exodus, the crossing of the Red Sea and the Jordan in Psalm 114:3, 4:

> The sea looked and fled,
> Jordan turned back,

The mountains skipped like rams,
the hills like lambs.

The figurative speech in this poem is related to the Canaanite literary technique which personalized natural forces into deities, but in this poem we have a good example of careful demythologizing, for the Hebrew article is employed on the words "sea" and "Jordan," to emphasize that they are not personal deity names. The Hebrews were certainly not unfamiliar with such Canaanite deity names as Yamm (Sea) and Nahar (River) as they appear in the Ras Shamra tablets. [107]

1. Paul W. Lapp, *The Dhahr Mirzbaneh Tombs,* ASOR Publications of the Jerusalem School, Archaeology: vol. IV. Similar finds were made at 'Ain Samiya, IEJ 21:75-85.

2. Nelson Glueck, *The River Jordan,* 2d ed., (1968), p. 116.

3. ANET, p. 329, no. 8. The "retainers" mentioned in this document are referred to next. See p. 328, n. 3.

4. The Ghassulian culture mentioned in the preceding chapter flourished in Chalcolithic times on the northern end of the Dead Sea. But this was more than a thousand years before the patriarchs.

5. The Madaba Mosaic Map and Eusebius' *Onomasticon;* cf. chapter VI; cf. E. G. Kraeling, Rand McNally Bible Atlas, pp. 70-72; also J. Penrose Harland, "Sodom and Gomorrah." 1. "The Location of the Cities of the Plain," BA 5:17-32, and 2. "The Destruction of the Cities of the Plain," BA 6:41-54.

6. W. F. Albright dates the sherds at Bab-ed-Dhra from the twenty-third to the twenty-first centuries (AP, pp. 77-78).

7. Kraeling, pp. 70-72.

8. R. E. Baney found what he claimed was a wall under water, (*Search for Sodom and Gomorrah,* Kansas City, Mo., 1963). More responsible underwater archaelogy was done by the Link Expedition, BA 24:50-59.

9. Shanhar *(Shin'ar)* is attested in Egyptian historical records as a name for part of Mesopotamia (cf. ANET, p. 247, n. 51).

10. Glueck and Aharoni prefer Tamar (see below, chap. 6, n.19). Kraeling suggests Wadi el-Ḥaṣaṣa near En-gedi, p. 68.

11. ANET, pp. 230-234, 554-555.

12. Kathleen Kenyon, *Archaeology in the Holy Land,* pp. 177-180.

13. Professor Moshe Kohavi, while excavating Tell Milḥ (Malḥata), informed me that this was true.

14. Kathleen Kenyon, *Digging Up Jericho,* pp. 249, 250.

15. ANET, p. 490.

16. ANET, pp. 242, 243.

17. AP, pp. 98-100.

18. ANET, p. 489, EA, no. 289.

19. ANET, p. 487, EA, no. 286.

20. ANET, p. 486, EA, no. 256.

21. H. J. Franken makes a case for a pottery break between Late Bronze Age and Early Iron Age as evidence for Israel's presence at Tell Deir Alla (*Excavations at Tell Deir Alla I,* Leiden, 1969) but no one would date Israel's arrival as late as the beginning of the twelfth century.

22. Such verses as Genesis 46:34 are in complete accord with Egyptian writings which express the same contempt for Asiatic herders.

23. "The 1968 Heshbon Expedition," BA 32:26-41.

24. Glueck believes Abel-shittim and Beth-jeshimoth were located in the higher land protecting the outlets of the wadies into the plains. He locates Abel-shittim at Tell Hammam. Beth-nimrah and Beth-haran of Numbers 32:36, which are called fenced cities, he locates at Bleibil and Tell Iktanu respectively (p. 204). But Joshua 13:27 locates them "in the valley" as part of the western border of Gad, along with the more northerly valley cities of Succoth and Zaphon (cf. Judg. 8:5-16; I Kings 7:46).

25. Kraeling, p. 124.

26. Kraeling, p. 126.

27. ANET, p. 320.

28. Kraeling, p. 126. J. Liver in "The Wars of Mesha, King of Moab" considers any identification of Beth-bamoth as conjectural, PEQ 98:17.

29. Ras Siyagha (Kraeling, p. 128).

30. Kraeling, p. 127.

31. Kraeling, p. 126.

32. I Kings 4:12 indicates that the district of Beth-shan bordered the district of Zarethan on the north. Numerous references to cities can be understood better when we realize that a great mother city often gave its name to the surrounding area. Aharoni prefers to locate Zarethan at Tell Umm Hamad, *The Land of the Bible* p. 31.

33. Kraeling, p. 133.

34. Kraeling, p. 133.

35. BASOR, no. 140, pp. 11-27.

36. Kenyon, *Archaeology in the Holy Land,* p. 198.

37. J. Garstang and J. B. E. Garstang, *The Story of Jericho.*

38. Kenyon, *Archaeology in the Holy Land,* p. 209.

39. Kenyon, p. 209.

40. Kenyon, p. 211.

41. Kenyon, *Digging Up Jericho,* p. 259.

42. D. W. Thomas, ed., p. 273.

43. AASOR 15:138; 18-19:268. Also, "Excavation of a Late Bronze Age Temple at Amman" (PEQ 98:155).

44. Kathleen Kenyon, *Amorites and Canaanites,* p. 64.

45. Kenyon, p. 5. Leon T. Wood gives a defense of the early date of the Exodus in *New Perspectives on the Old Testament,* pp. 66-87.

46. IEJ, 19:121-123.

47. ANET, p. 329, n. 8.

48. *Archives Royales de Mari,* 6 (1954):39, 111.

49. ANET, p. 242.

50. ANET, p. 477.

51. "The year after Simuru and Lulubu were destroyed for the ninth time" (N. Schneider, "Die Zeitbestimmungen der Wirtschaftsurkunden von Ur III," *Analecta Orientalia,* no. 13, p. 52).

52. ANEP, no. 460. A similar symbol is on the Bar Rebub Stela from Zenjirli which is inscribed in honor of Baal of Haran, a center of moon worship. For additional information on Hazor see Y. Yadin, *Hazor I-IV,* 1958-61.

53. Albright, AP, p. 103. See Numbers 34:11; Deuteronomy 3:17; Joshua 11:2; 12:3; 13:27; 19:35; I Kings 15:20 show the city was a fenced fortress according to Joshua 19:35 and gave its name to the Sea of Galilee and that entire region according to I Kings 15:20.

54. ANET, p. 249. The stela may be seen in the Palestine Archaeological Museum in Jerusalem. See A. Rowe, *The Topography and History of Beth-shan, I,* Pl. 33. Also ANEP Pl. 487 and *Mekal, the God of Beth-shan,* H.O. Thompson.

55. Kenyon, *Amorites and Canaanites,* p. 3.

56. Albright, AP, p. 105; ANET, p. 253. The 17th Annual Convention of the Israel Exploration Society was on "The Valley of Beth-shan," (IEJ 11:198).

57. Paul W. Lapp, "Palestine: Known But Mostly Unknown" BA 26:125. The 1963 Wooster Expedition to Pella was in cooperation with the American Schools of Oriental Research. Most of the material excavated was from the Byzantine Period. See the *Wooster Alumni Magazine,* January 1968.

58. ANET, p. 253, n. 6.

59. AASOR 6:14, 22, 23.

60. ANET, p. 253, n. 7. Wherever Yanoam was, it was a town surrounded by a forest. This fact we learn from the scenes on the north exterior wall of the great hypostyle hall at Karnak, where Seti shows in pictures his military activities by which he sought to reconstitute the Empire (ANEP, pp. 106-110).

61. ANET, p. 477. Qiyen and Tirqa-El cannot yet be identified.

62. ANET, p. 255.

63. ANET, p. 255, n. 3.

64. ANET, pp. 256-258. Ramses II claimed victories from Southern Palestine to Northern Syria (ANET, p. 256, B).

65. ANET, p. 262, 263.

66. J. A. Wilson, *The Culture of Ancient Egypt*, p. 259.

67. ANET, p. 262, n. 21.

68. Another twelfth century stela from Beth-shan shows how eclectic Egyptians were at this time. An Egyptian ruler Hesi-Nekbt tells of his worship of the Canaanite goddess "Antit, queen of heaven, mistress of all gods." He writes in hieroglyphs, worships a Canaanite goddess, and uses Aegean pottery. The document is in the Palestine Archaeological Museum in East Jerusalem.

69. Kenyon, *Digging Up Jericho*, p. 263.

70. Here we follow Y. Aharoni, *The Land of the Bible*, p. 241, n. 172. Twenty Hebrew manuscripts have Zeredah instead of Zererah. Aharoni takes Zeredah to be Zarethan. This is likely because of the identification of the two spellings in I Kings 7:46 and II Chronicles 4:17. If Zererah is the correct reading then the place might be Tell el-Mezar, with the original name Zerer reflected in nearby Darar.

71. The mouth of the Jordan is a tongue of alluvial land which juts out into the Dead Sea where the Jordan River enters (Josh. 15:5).

72. Hajla near Beth-abara which, according to John 1:28, was beside *(peran)* to the Jordan where John was baptizing.

73. Gideon was rebuffed by the princes of Succoth when he begged sustenance for his men. The reason they gave is not readily understood by the average reader. "Are the hands of Zebah and Zalmunna now in thine hand, that we should give bread unto thine army?" (Judg. 8:6 KJV). The custom of cutting off hands as trophies of war may be seen on the walls of the mortuary temple of Ramses III at Medinet Habu (ANEP, 118). The RSV obscures this meaning of the verse by taking liberty with the Hebrews and the New English Bible does no better.

74. These fords are: Sayida, Umm Sidra, Abu Sidra, and Turkumaniya.

75. Kraeling, p. 278; Glueck prefers Tell el-Maqlub near the Wadi

Yabis (pp. 136-138). Y. Aharoni suggests Khirbet Tell el-Hilu (p. 241, n. 172).

76. A. Rowe, *Beth-shan, Four Canaanite Temples*. ANEP, Pls. 732, 736-738.

77. Kenyon, *Archaeology in the Holy Land*, p. 231. Aharoni suggests that the battle of Mount Gilboa was necessary from the Philistine viewpoint in order for them to control the *Via Maris* which passed by Beth-shan and up the Jezreel Valley (p. 258).

78. These anthropoid clay coffins were used in Egypt and in Palestine from the Late Bronze Age on, but they are usually found with Philistine pottery (Albright, AP, pp. 115-117; Kenyon, *Archaeology in the Holy Land*, p. 227; ANEP, Pl. 641).

79. The Egyptians had used Sea Peoples as mercenaries since the Amarna Age. The Sherden who were related to the Philistines formed part of the Egyptian garrison in Palestine in Amarna times and subsequent kings numbered them among their troops (Kenyon, *Archaeology in the Holy Land*, p. 227; ANET, pp. 255, 260, 476).

80. As noted in Chapter 2, footnote 12, this is another case where the Hebrew *'ēber* should be rendered "along" or "adjacent to," not "the other side."

81. Glueck, pp. 130-136.

82. The southern coastal region where five Philistine tyrants controlled the cities of Ashdod, Ashkelon, Gaza, Gath, and Ekron.

83. Glueck, *The River Jordan* pp. 126-129; as noted Aharoni prefers Tell Umm Hamad for Zarethan (p. 31).

84. James B. Pritchard, "The First Excavations at Tell es-Sa'idiyeh" BA 28:10-17.

85. The laver is called in the Hebrew of I Kings 7:26 *yam* (a sea). Some suggest this has mythological associations (G. E. Wright, *Biblical Archaeology*, p. 140) because of the Canaanite Sea God, Yamm. Any sizable body of water, even a river, might be called a *yam* in Hebrew.

86. The Israelis today have a copper plant there extracting the ore by a wet chemical method.

87. Beno Rothenberg, "Ancient Copper Industries in the Western Arabah," PEQ 94 (1962): 5-71. More recently Rothenberg has discovered that the Edomites were mining copper in the southern Arabah at Wadi Mene'iyeh as early as the thirteenth century (Aharoni, p. 189; p. 174, n. 47).

88. Glueck, "Ezion-geber," BA 28-70-87.

89. There seems to be considerable difference of opinion about Solomon's use of this ore. Glueck still maintains that Solomon obtained a considerable part of his wealth from this industry (Glueck, BA 28:73).

90. Aharoni believes Tell Deir Alla is still the best candidate for Succoth although Franken suggests nearby Tell el-Ekhsas. The destruction which is evident on the mound from early in the twelfth century, Aharoni believes, could be the work of Gideon (p. 241; p. 242, n. 174). See Franken, *Excavations at Deir Alla* and *Vetus Testamentum* 10:386, 11:361, 12:378, 14:417.

91. Aharoni, pp. 114, 115.

92. The Amarna tablets inform us that a certain Labayu controlled all the central hill country north of Jerusalem to Shechem. He had sons, one of whom was Mut-Baalu of Pella. The princess of Zaphon complained to the Egyptian king of the Apiru (Habiru) who were harassing her city. The Apiru were friends, perhaps even the sons, of Labayu. (BASOR 89:15-17).

93. Aharoni, pp. 278-280. ANEP, Pl. 349.

94. Glueck, p. 139; G. A. Smith, *The Historical Geography of the Holy Land*, p. 318, nn. 1 and 2.

95. I. M. Blake (PEQ 99:86-97) attempts to deal with Joshua's curse and Elisha's miracle on the basis of temporary lethal quantities of radioactivity in the water. His arguments are rebutted by E. Mazor (PEQ 101:46, 47).

96. *Time Magazine*, 81:44, April 19, 1963. Denis Baly tells of "the menace of sudden flash floods from the highlands of the Khurashe Dome . . . " (*The Geography of the Bible*, p. 216).

97. Some think the enemy crossed to En-gedi on boats but this seems unlikely for these were not boat-building people (Baly, p. 207). It is very likely that they waded across at the Lisan, which was possible in ancient times. (Aharoni, p. 32).

98. G. A. Smith points out that the Roman map Tabula Pentingeriana shows such a road in Roman times which was probably built along the ancient "way of the Reed Sea" (IEJ 4:9-16).

99. Nelson Glueck, "The Civilization of the Edomites" in *The Biblical Archaeologist Reader*, ed. Edward F. Campbell, Jr., and David Noel Freedman (Garden City, New York, 1964), 2:56.

100. Sela is believed to be Umm el Biyara, a flat topped rock fortress around which Petra grew. (*Deities and Dolphins*, N. Glueck, p. 43).

101. Glueck, *"The Civilization of the Edomites,"* p. 58. Glueck also found a seal at Ezion-geber (Kheleifeh) bearing the name Jotham, a possible reference to the son of Uzziah who also controlled the Edomites.

102. Even elephants inhabited Palestine, especially in the Jordan Valley in prehistoric times. Elephant tusks have been found near the bridge of the "Daughters of Jacob" north of the Sea of Galilee (Glueck, *The River Jordan*, p. 22).

103. ANET, p. 242.

104. ANET, p. 307, n. 1.

105. *The Anchor Bible,* 16, Psalms I, p. 258.

106. In the Ugaritic mythology Baal goes hunting for buffalo in the Shimak Canebrake which H. L. Ginsberg thinks may be Semachonitis (Lake Huleh). (ANET, p. 142).

107. In Ugaritic, *Nahar* and *Yamm* were two of the epithets for that deity, Baal, who controlled these forces of nature (ANET, pp. 130, 131).

5 Intertestamental and New Testament Times

Except for certain sites in and along the valley where considerable excavation has been carried on, such as Jericho, Masada, and Qumran, our knowledge of the Jordan Valley in this period is more tantalizing than satisfying. Important literary sources of information on the Jordan Valley at this time are the New Testament, Josephus, and the books of I and II Maccabees. Many details of Josephus' account of the Jewish War of 66-72 A.D. have been upheld by the excavations at Masada.[1] The Dead Sea Scrolls found since 1948 in the Judean wilderness represent the most significant of all archaeological discoveries ever made in Palestine. The scrolls are especially important for textual criticism of the Old Testament and for Jewish religion and history in the first centuries before and after Christ. For the first few centuries A.D. the geography of Palestine, including part of the Jordan Valley, is illuminated by the Madaba Mosaic Map (late sixth century A.D.) and by Eusebius' Onomasticon (fourth century A.D.).[2]

Significant events in the Gospels center around the Lake of Galilee, the Jordan River, and the Jericho area. John the Baptist's ministry, like that of Elijah and Elisha, was closely associated with the Jordan Valley. Considering the size of the Gospels, these events represent a considerable portion of the

109

The Qumran caves in the Judean wilderness. Cave 4, marked by a circle in the photograph, contained what seems to have been the bulk of the library of the Qumran Community.

ministry of Jesus. Certainly the Jordan Valley was a familiar sight to him. Jesus lived as a boy in the southern hills of Galilee overlooking the valley of Esdraelon. The bustling commercial activity in the lake towns and in the busy Decapolis city of Scythopolis (Beth-shan) must have been felt daily in the little hamlet called Nazareth, although the town was not exactly on any major route. The road coming from Damascus went across the Jordan Valley a little below the Lake of Galilee and then continued west via Sepphoris (north of Nazareth) to Ptolemais (Acco) on the Mediterranean. The road also went on south in the Jordan Valley to Scythopolis and then west up the valley of Esdraelon or on south in the Jordan Valley to Jericho. The latter was an especially pleasant way to make the trip from Galilee to Jerusalem in winter. It was a route Jesus sometimes took (Luke 19:1).

John the Baptist went in all the "region about Jordan preaching the baptism of repentance" (Luke 3:3). The phrase "region about Jordan" was a familiar term for the floor of the Jordan Valley, the *Ghor*. The New English Bible translates this verse: "And he went all over the Jordan Valley proclaiming a baptism . . . ." The fact that John preached on the eastern as well as the western side made it possible for Herod Antipas to arrest him, for Herod's domain, Perea, was on the eastern side. John the Evangelist (1:28) tells us that the Baptist baptized Jesus at "Bethany beyond Jordan." The statement tells us nothing about whether this Bethany was on the east or west side of the Jordan because the Greek text can mean "Bethany alongside the Jordan." Since there is no known Bethany in the Jordan Valley the reading of some ancient manuscripts which give Bethabara for Bethany should be considered a possibility. Of course it is always possible that there was a Bethany about which nothing is known.[3] This is possible but unlikely, since the church father, Origen, who preferred the reading Bethabara, knew of no Bethany in the Jordan Valley. Some believe that Bethabara was an error for Betharabah of Joshua 15:6. Others feel it should be connected with Beth-barah of Judges 7:24 which has practically the same spelling as Bethabara.[4] Bethabara which means literally "fordtown," was north of the Hajlah ford, which is the traditional spot where Jesus was baptized by John.

The Arabah, Petra, and the Nabateans

In Hellenistic times a significant political development which was to affect the Rift Valley was the rise of the Nabatean kingdom. Their greatest king, Aretas IV (9 B.C.-40 A.D.), was in control of Damascus when Paul escaped, being let down from the city wall in a basket (II Cor. 11:33; Acts 9:25). The fortress of Macherus just north of the great Arnon cleft, overlooking the northeastern corner of the Dead Sea, usually marked the Nabatean northern boundary. For a time this border separated the tetrarchy of Herod Antipas and the Nabatean kingdom. The Nabateans, a bedouin people had driven the Edomites from their ancient home into southern Judea, which then became Idumea. Alexander Jannaeus (B.C.

The Treasury is one of the most perfectly preserved monuments at Petra. Hellenic in style, it is an imposing royal tomb hewn out of the rose-red rock by the Nabateans.

104-178) conquered Idumea and Judaized it. Herod the Great, an Idumean, had no love for the Nabateans; nor did Herod Antipas, who broke his alliance with them by divorcing the daughter of Aretas. As a result Antipas was defeated by the Nabateans and shortly thereafter went into exile. Nabatean inscriptions are in Greek and Aramaic, the latter being in unique script used only by them. The Nabateans became wealthy because they controlled those ancient trade routes from Arabia to the Mediterranean and Syria which had been so important to the Edomites and Hebrews in Old Testament times. Although their domain was primarily what had been Edom and Moab, they briefly controlled Damascus, the northern Arabah, and part of the Negev.

The Seleucid Antigonus is the first to mention the Nabateans in his conquests of 312 B.C.[5] Early mention is also made in the Apocrypha, where we learn that the Nabateans were friends of the Maccabees, who occasionally sought refuge with them (II Macc. 5:8). One such episode involved the Jordan Valley. When Jonathan the brother of Judas became leader of the Maccabees, the Jews, who were using guerrilla warfare, were forced to send their personal belongings over to the friendly Nabateans. Near Madaba the party carrying this baggage was ambushed by robbers who slew John Maccabeus. Jonathan and Simon crossed the Jordan to avenge their brother's blood but on their return were met in the Jordan Valley by general Bacchides and a Syrian army. On this occasion the Maccabean heroes saved themselves by swimming the Jordan and disappearing into the wilderness of Judea.[6]

The Nabateans carved magnificent Hellenistic and Roman architectural facades in the beautiful variegated red and yellow sandstone mountains which line the eastern side of the Arabah at Petra. The Wadi Musa collects water from the highlands surrounding Petra, and then flows northward in the Arabah but eventually sinks into the arid land before it can reach the Dead Sea. Petra became an important caravan city because it had the most abundant water supply between Hejaz[7] and Palestine. A very narrow passage between cliffs three hundred feet high, called the Siq, provides entrance

Nabatean ware.

Nabatean inscriptions at Petra.

into a valley where the city of Petra is situated. The well-protected city within the valley had a Roman theater, numerous shrines, temples, gates, and private homes which give evidence of the rich material culture of the Nabateans. They are noted for a very thin, delicately painted red pottery, and were skilled in hydraulic engineering, as is evidenced by highly developed techniques in building terraces and dams for storing sparse but torrential desert rains. Otherwise this water would quickly disappear and leave the land parched in the dry season. A first century Nabatean sanctuary on top of Jebel et-Tannur along the Wadi Zered showed that the Nabateans at this point were using the name Zeus-Hadad instead of the native name Dusares for their chief deity.[8] The Nabateans controlled the Arabah and the Negev until Petra was destroyed by Trajan about 106 A.D. In the second century A.D. the city of Petra flourished again but Nabatean domain was now part of the Roman Provincia Arabia.

Macherus and Masada

Josephus says that the Maccabean ruler Alexander Jannaeus built up the fortress called Macherus near the northeastern shore of the Dead Sea on a high peak with deep ravines around it.[9] It was originally intended as a fort against Nabatean encroachment. Herod the Great made the fortress even more imposing by putting in towers and strong walls. Following his Roman inclination for an abundant water supply he dug many cisterns, as he did at all his citadels.[10] Later Herod Antipas attempted to use Macherus as a border fortress against the Nabateans. The fortress apparently changed hands several times. It was here, according to Josephus, that John the Baptist was held prisoner before he was beheaded for condemning Herod's marriage to Herodias, his brother's wife (Matt. 14:1-12). By rejecting his wife, Harith, the daughter of Aretas IV, Antipas offended the Nabateans and brought an end to an already unstable peace agreement.[11] During the war of 66-72 A.D. Jewish zealots held out at Macherus after the fall of Jerusalem, as they did at Masada on the western shore, but Bassus, the Roman

general, persuaded them to surrender the citadel by threaten-
ing to crucify one of their captured heroes. The bargain was
supposed to guarantee their freedom but Josephus says that
later Bassus marched his soldiers to the forest of the Jordan
(the *Zor*) where many Jews who had escaped from Jerusalem
and Macherus were in hiding. A pitched battle ensued, the
Romans cut down trees to expose their enemy, and three
thousand Jews were slaughtered.[12]

On the western side of the Dead Sea, eleven miles south of
En-gedi, another mountain redoubt overlooking the Jordan
Valley was made into a luxurious citadel by Herod the Great.
It was called Masada, "the fortress" in Aramaic. Josephus
also speaks vividly of events involving this fortress in the
Jewish War of 66-72 A.D.[13] His account was largely vindi-
cated by the Israeli excavations led by Y. Yadin.[14] The
fortress is much more imposing than Macherus, having a sheer
drop of one thousand feet on its eastern side. On the top of
the mountain Herod built a refuge for his household in case
of revolt or siege from his many enemies. Here Herod included an imposing water system capable of collecting and
storing up to a million and a half gallons of water. As a result
he was able to build Roman baths, fountains, and pools in his
refuge.

After Herod the Great's death the elaborately columned
palaces and storehouses fell progressively into disuse. Sometime during the first century A.D. the Romans stationed a
detachment of soldiers at Masada. This detachment was there
prior to the outbreak of the Jewish revolt in 66 A.D. The
revolt started when the Jewish zealots under the leadership of
Menahem ben Judah of Galilee seized the fortress by surprise
and used it as a base against the Roman army. After the fall
of Jerusalem in 70 A.D. the zealots determined to make
Masada their last stand. With plenty of food and water they
held out until it was evident that the Roman Tenth Legion
would reach them using a massive causeway built with slave
labor acquired from the fall of Jerusalem. Seeing their cause
lost, some nine hundred zealots, men, women, and children,
chose to die by their own hands rather than fall slaves to the
Roman army. Josephus records the impassioned speech de-

Above: Looking down on the ruins of Herod's palace at Masada. Right: Corinthian capital from Herod's palace. Below: A view of the excavations at Masada.

livered by their leader Eleazer Ben Yair before they carried out the bloody task against their own women and children and themselves.[15] Yadin's excavations at Masada were exceedingly fruitful. New scrolls were found containing both Biblical and non-Biblical texts including a scroll which contained the lost Hebrew original of the Book of Jubilees. Many inscribed sherds and a large quantity of coins were among the treasures found.

The Wilderness of Judea

A much-publicized site which bordered the Jordan Valley in Hellenistic and New Testament times is Khirbet Qumran, the home of the people who produced the Dead Sea Scrolls. This "monastery" was just north of the perennial spring at Wadi Feshkha which its people used for irrigation farming and as a source of fresh fish. It should be noted that the Judean wilderness, including all the barren hills bordering the valley south of Wadi Fariah, have become important archaeologically because of the relative dryness which tends to preserve perishable materials if they are protected from the combined effect of the sun and occasional torrential rain. Hence, caves have yielded undreamed-of quantities of documents made of leather and papyrus. Even when badly fragmented these are treasures indeed for Palestine, where the archaeologist finds comparatively little written material. In recent years, with the help of bedouin like the Taamireh tribe who found the original scrolls, new documents keep coming to light.[16]

Fragmented documents now called the Samarian Papyri, with coins, sealings, etc., were found in a cave in the Wadi Daliyeh, eight or nine miles north of Jericho and seven or eight miles west of the Jordan, in the barren hills of the western fault. These documents date from pre-Alexandrine times (375-335 B.C.). The contents are written in an Aramaic cursive script and in Paleo-Hebrew. Though fragmentary they

Ruins of the monastery at Qumran.

portend to shed considerable light on this otherwise little-known period in Palestine. According to F. Cross the scripts used in these papyri confirm the third century B.C. dating for some of the manuscripts from Qumran.[17]

Qarn Sartabeh, anciently called Alexandrium, and Khirbet Mird (ancient Hyrcania) are two fortresses in this area which were originally built by Armenians but destroyed by the Roman general Gabinius at the time of Pompey's conquest (63 B.C.).[18] Herod the Great restored them along with Macherus and Masada and used Hyrcania as a prison for political offenders. Its ruins have yielded Byzantine manuscripts, while excavations in Wadi Buqe'ah to the east of Mird but west of Qumran have yielded considerable Iron II materials.[19] Early fortresses in this region appear to be the Biblical sites of Joshua 15:61, 62, Middin, Secacah, and Nibshan. The city of the Salt (Sea) mentioned in these verses may be Khirbet Qumran itself, since excavations there show an Iron II fortress under the Essene remains. This could be related to the fortresses built by Jehoshaphat recorded in II Chronicles 17:12.

Another wadi which reaches the Dead Sea from the west as a deep gorge is Wadi Murabba'at. Here French scholars found caves full of important materials from the Jewish guerrilla warfare of the Second Revolt of A.D. 132-135, including fragments of the Old Testament and the correspondence of the Jewish warriors. Even a copy of Simeon ben Kosibah's Declaration of the Revolt was discovered.[20]

Perea

Perea was a strip of territory along the eastern side of the Jordan Valley which was hemmed in by the Nabateans to the south and the Decapolis to the north and east. After the death of Herod the Great a Jew named Simon, a former slave of Herod, collected a band and declared himself king of Perea. He was soon conquered and put to death. Due to general revolt throughout the land Varus, the governor of Syria, was obliged to march up and down apprehending the rebels. He crucified some two thousand Jews. In the time of Christ, Herod Antipas controlled Perea and Galilee as tetrarch, which made him a little less than a king. For the defense of Perea against the Nabateans, Antipas fortified the Perean city of Beth-aramphtha, the Old Testament city Beth-haram (Num. 32:36 and Josh. 13:27) in the plains of Moab. The city had been burned in Simon's revolt. When it was rebuilt by Antipas he called it Livias in honor of the Emperor Augustus's wife. Later, in keeping with a change in her name, it was called Julias, but none of these names survived among the local people, who still call the site after its ancient name Tell er-Rameh (Harem).

Josephus says Placides, one of Vespasian's generals, "took Abila, Julias, and Bezemoth" and "all that lay as far as the lake Asphaltites."[21] Abila is undoubtedly Old Testament Abel-shittim (Num. 33:49) and is connected both by archaeology and the literature with Khirbet Kefrein on the north side of the Wadi Kefrein (also called Wadi Hesban). As noted, Julias is er-Rameh, while Bezemoth is the same name as Beth-jeshimoth of Numbers 33:49. Archaeologists locate the Old Testament Beth-jeshimoth at Tell Azeimeh, while a nearby Hellenistic-Roman town, Bezemoth (Isimuth) is a little closer to the Dead Sea at Khirbet Sweimeh.[22]

If we move now south along the eastern shore of the Dead Sea we arrive at a gorge called Zerqa Ma'in, where waters from a hot spring drop over a falls shortly before entering the Dead Sea. This seems to be the hot springs of Callirhoe where Herod the Great often bathed for curative purposes. If Herod was carried to this spring by boat the falls would have made it difficult to reach the spring itself. Therefore D. Baly prefers to locate Callirhoe at a place designated Zara on the northeastern shore where the ruins of a fort, shown on the Madaba Map, still stand.[23]

New Testament Jericho

The Jordan Valley around the Jericho oasis was always beloved by Palestinians especially as a winter resort area.

The oasis at Jericho as viewed from the site of Old Testament Jericho.

Herod the Great was never one to miss an opportunity to build a luxury palace in a favored spot. Herodian Jericho was excavated by J. L. Kelso and J. B. Pritchard in 1950 and 1951.[24] The New Testament Jericho was located about one mile west of the modern town on the bank of Wadi Qelt at Tulul Abu el-'Alayiq. In 1950 excavations here brought to light a type of Roman masonry thought to be used only in Italy. The stones were laid in mortar to form a net-like pattern called *opus reticulatum*. This pattern may be seen in many of the walls and buildings in Italy, especially at Pompeii and Herculaneum.

New Testament Jericho was a lavish Roman city, the winter capital of Herod with terraced gardens, pools, expensive villas, Roman baths, a great gymnasium, theaters, and a hippodrome. None of the *opus reticulatum* type masonry was found in a building excavated by Pritchard a year later (1951). Kelso attributed the *opus reticulatum* work to the period of Herod's son Archelaus. Herod's winter capital was on both sides of the Wadi Qelt. There were private villas and public buildings, some with walls over three feet thick. Greek and Roman plays were staged in a large sunken garden 350

Falls in Wadi Zerqa Ma'in, assumed by some experts to be the hot springs of Callirhoe.

feet long. At one end of the garden a stairway thirteen feet wide went up 150 feet to a building which had foundations dating back to a Maccabean fort.[25] The water from Wadi Qelt supplied a gymnasium 170' by 145' including quarters for army personnel. An amphitheater and a hippodrome are mentioned in the literature but were not excavated. Balsam groves in the New Testament Jericho were so valuable that Mark Antony gave the city to Cleopatra as a prized gift. After Augustus defeated Antony, Cleopatra committed suicide and Herod persuaded Augustus to give back to him the district of Jericho along with other important centers like Hippos east of the Lake of Galilee.[26] Herod also built an entirely new city between Jericho and the mountain fortress, Alexandrium. He named the city Phasaelis after his brother who had lost his life in the Parthian invasion about 40 B.C. Eventually the city of Archelais immediately north of Jericho was built. In Roman times this whole area, normally very dry, flourished due to Roman aqueducts which spread available water over a wide area.[27]

A mountain citadel above New Testament Jericho on the south bank of Wadi Qelt was called Kypros. Herod the Great gave this stronghold to his mother. The pottery at the site, especially one type of globular juglet, resembles closely ware found at Qumran. Some fragments of the finest ware of the Roman Period, called "Pergamene" ware, proves rich people lived here. Cooking pots, Roman sigillata ware, Herodian lamps, and pilgrim flasks with two twisted handles are like those of the same period at Jerusalem.

Coins at Alayiq prove this occupation dates from Herod's reign (37-4 B.C.) and continued until the end of the reign of Herod Agrippa I (37-44 A.D.). Josephus identified the complex as Herod's winter palace.[28] He tells how the rebellious Jew Simon, who had proclaimed himself king after Herod's death, burned this royal palace at Jericho .

North of Damiyeh

Among other important sites which bordered the northern Jordan Valley in New Testament times was the city of Pella (pp. 19, 76, 77, 137). It was located on the eastern side of the valley just north of Wadi Yabis and Wadi Jurm. The ruins in the eastern foothills, called by the Arabs today Tabaqat Fahl, are the ancient Pahel and first century Pella. Excavations by the Wooster Expedition made a sounding at Pella in 1958.[29] The most ostensible ruins are Roman and the Wooster group plans to excavate nearby Tell Husn, where great Roman structures are very evident. We have mentioned that Egyptian records and the Amarna letters reckon with the importance of this city, but it played no role in the Bible (pp. 54, 55, 107). We do know that the city was rebuilt after the time of Alexander the Great and its name was Grecized from Pahel to Pella. The city was destroyed again by Alexander Jannaeus but in 63 B.C. the Roman general Pompey gave it freedom as an independent city of the province of Syria, and soon after it became part of the commercial league of ten cities known as the Decapolis. In New Testament times Pella was connected by a road to its sister cities. When the Jewish revolt broke out in 66 A.D. the Christians of the city of Jerusalem fled to Pella (Luke 21:20, 21), which then became a Christian center for a long time. The second century Christian apologist Aristo came from Pella; it was so important in Byzantine times (450 A.D.) that the city had its own bishop.

According to excavation records, following the attack by the Egyptian Shishak in 918 B.C., Beth-shan lay in ruins until Hellenistic times (I Kings 14:25).[30] For some reason the city re-emerged under the name Scythopolis. The Septuagint translation of Judges 1:27 mentions Beth-shan and adds the words "which is the city of the Scythians" (*skython polis*). [31] Herodotus implies that the Scythians created an empire which included Palestine, but there is no evidence for this. Glueck presents the idea that a certain type of twisted collar found on Nabatean idols can be traced to the Scythians via the Parthians. Since Scythians formed the chief part of Parthian military strength they continued their influence in the Near East long after their heyday. So it may have been Scythian-Parthians who continued as military overlords in Beth-shan well into the Hellenistic and Roman periods.[32]

When the Roman general Pompey turned against the Mac-

cabean prince Aristobulus II (69-63 B.C.) the Jordan Valley was destined to play a role in the events which followed. Pompey pursued Aristobulus from Dium (Dion), a city of the Decapolis located somewhere north or south of the Yarmuk in Bashan.[33] From here Pompey passed Pella as he crossed the valley near Scythopolis and proceeded south in the *Ghor* to the verdant Wadi Faria, which joins the Jordan near Damiyeh. High on the rugged western scarp at this point was located the fortress Alexandrium (Qarn Sartaba), to which Aristobulus had fled. After many negotiations the fortress was surrendered but Aristobulus went on to Jerusalem, there to prepare to resist the Roman army. Pompey pursued him down the Jordan Valley to Jericho and thence to Jerusalem where he laid siege to the city. Later the victorious Pompey put all the non-Jewish towns in and adjacent to the Jordan Valley, such as Hippos, Pella, and Scythopolis, under the rule of the governor of Syria which was then made a Roman province.[34]

The Valley near the Lake of Galilee

Not very much is known about the cities which Jesus visited on the shores of the Lake of Galilee. For years it was thought that a ruin called Khan Minyeh was Capernaum, but excavations of a second century A.D. synagogue at Tell Hum and a statement by the pilgrim Theodosium (530 A.D.) have made Hum a more likely location.[35] Both sites are on the northwestern shore of the lake. The New Testament mentions a synagogue at Capernaum where Jesus taught (Luke 4:31). Luke says that a building, possibly this very synagogue, had been erected in Capernaum by a centurion who loved Judaism and later believed in Jesus (Luke 7:5). It is more likely that the first century building is underneath the second or third century synagogue now in evidence at Tell Hum. The earliest synagogue excavated in Galilee and one of

Ruins of a second century A.D. synagogue at Tell Hum.

the earliest in Palestine was unearthed at the hot springs of Emmaus (Hammath) immediately south of Tiberias.[36]

The synagogue at Capernaum is about 70 feet by 50 feet, very elaborately ornamented, representing a liberal Jewish view toward artistic embellishment. Figures of animals and people are in sharp contrast to the practice of those post-exilic Jews who held an extreme interpretation of the second commandment (Exod. 20:4). The building is constructed of white limestone which had to be carried some distance to this place. It is a Roman basilica with colonnaded hall and court. Some pillars of the building are inscribed with the names of donors. It is interesting that the name Capernaum (City of Nahum) is not mentioned in these inscriptions at Tell Hum (Nahum). But the name is mentioned in inscriptions at another synagogue in the Jordan Valley. An Aramaic memorial at an old synagogue in Hamath Geder (el Hammeh), at the mouth of the Yarmuk, mentions Kaphar Nahum (the city of Nahum).[37] Excavations by V. Corbo at Capernaum in 1968 unearthed a fisherman's house dating to the first century A.D. As early as the second century the building was used by Christians as a *domus ecclesia* (a private home where early Christians met for prayer and worship). By the fifth century an octagonal basilical church was erected over the home. Corbo firmly believes that this was Saint Peter's house referred to in Mark (1:29, 33).[38] Josephus also says that he was taken to Capernaum to recuperate after he was thrown from his horse in the course of a battle against a Roman detachment in the Jordan Valley not far from Julias.[39] This Julias, also called Bethsaida, was located just east of the entrance of the Jordan into the Lake of Galilee.[40] No excavation has been done at the site but it is probably Khirbet el-Araj. Roman remains to go back to the time of Pilate and some evidence indicates the city was later put to the flame, which would be in fulfillment of Jesus' malediction on the city (Matt. 11:21).[41] Jesus at Bethsaida in Mark 8:22 healed a blind man in two stages. E. G. Kraeling notes that Bethsaida is called here a "village." He therefore believes that it was the lake-port village connected with the larger city Bethsaida which the Tetrarch Philip built up and renamed "Julias." The point is well taken, for Pliny puts Julias on the east bank of the river and Josephus says it was near the junction of a river and a lake. The city then would be et-Tell, a mile inland from the lake and Mark's village at el-Araj, where pottery and coins from the time of Christ have been found. Caesarea Philippi on the slopes of Hermon was the Tetrarch Philip's summer home, while Julias was his winter home in the Jordan Valley.

Tiberias, in the middle of the western shore of the Lake, a most beautiful spot near the hot springs of Emmaus, was built by Herod Antipas as a capital. The city was started during the reign of the emperor Tiberias (ca. 18 A.D.), hence the name. A tradition persists that the Jews were offended because Herod built it on the site of a cemetery, which made it difficult for observing Jews to live there because it occasioned ceremonial impurity for them. Some Jews would not enter the city. Herod had to import foreigners to inhabit his capital. Later in the third century it became a center of Jewish learning. A royal palace and many beautiful public structures were built in the city. The lake is called by the evangelist John the Sea of Tiberias (6:1; 21:1) but otherwise the city is mentioned only once in the New Testament (John 6:23).

A little to the north of Tiberias and immediately to the south of the plain of Gennesaret (Ginnesar, or el-Ghuweir) is located Magdala (Mejdel), the home of Mary "Magdalene" (Matt. 27:56, Mark 15:40). Josephus calls it Tarichaea,[42] a name it acquired during Hellenistic times. Josephus had the city's walls rebuilt and estimates the population at about 40,000 in 70 A.D. Some believe Magadan (Matt. 15:39) and Dalmanutha (Mark 8:10) are simply different ways of referring to Magdal. In the plain of Gennesaret Jesus performed an outstanding healing miracle after He had walked on the waters and brought His disciples safely to land (Matt. 14:34; Mark 6:53). According to the Aramaic version of Numbers 34:11, Ginnesar is the Aramaic pronunciation of the Old Testament town Chinnereth, which gave the lake its Old

Testament name.[43] Chinnereth lay in ruins in New Testament times. It was situated on a hill overlooking the junction of the road by which one may go either south along the lake to Capernaum or north away from the lake to the "Bridge of the Daughters of Jacob." Capernaum and Chinnereth lay along the important route Via Maris (Way of the Sea). Matthew 4:15, 16 quotes Isaiah 9:1: "The land of Zabulon, and the land of Nephthali, by the way of the sea, beyond Jordan, Galilee of the Gentiles; The people which sat in darkness saw a great light . . . ." The reference here to "the way of the sea" is to the part of the Via Maris which went by the Lake of Galilee. The route which went from Damascus by Hazor along the Lake of Galilee was indeed part of the major Via Maris road which continued down the Jordan Valley to Scythopolis (Beth-shan) and west to the Megiddo pass and then along the Mediterranean to Egypt. That it went by the lake as well as by the waters of the Great Sea fits the Hebrew usage of the word *yam* (sea) by which one may refer to any sizable body of water. As we have noted before, "beyond Jordan" can be translated "adjacent to Jordan" (pp. 25, 30, 31). The Hebrew 'ēber (Isa. 9:1) and the Greek *peran* (Matt. 4:15) can mean "adjacent to"; these areas were not on the eastern side as "beyond" suggests.

Near Tell Hum is et-Tabgha, where beautiful mosaics on the floor of the Byzantine Heptapegon (the Seven Springs) Church depict Christ's miracle of the loaves and fishes. Mosaic scenes of the Nile River show a Nilometer, a tower for measuring the depth of the Nile's flood each year. But it appears the feeding of the five thousand (Matt. 14:15-21) took place in a lonely place somewhat more removed from these cities on the western shore. Some believe that Tabgha with its springs and excellent fishing "grounds" was the New Testament Bethsaida (Mark 8:22-26), which means the House of Fishing. But the only evidence for this is the excellent fishing near this spot. If the home of Peter,

Structure from Roman times, containing a flour mill, located on the shores of Lake Galilee near Magdala.

Ruins of a synagogue at Chorazin.

Andrew, and Philip (John 1:44, 12:21) should not be identified with Bethsaida-Julias on the northeastern shore, then
another location must be found, because no city remains
have been found at Tabgha.

Moving again to the northern end of the lake we come to Chorazin (Matt. 11:21-23), another one of the Galilean cities which Jesus rebuked along with Capernaum and Bethsaida. The Arabs call it Keraze, and it is about two miles north of Capernaum but somewhat more removed from the shore. A second or third century synagogue here is made of the local black lava rock. Among the richly adorned sculptures of animals and festival scenes, there is a seat of honor reminding us of "the seat of Moses" mentioned in Matthew 23:2. The front of the seat has an inscription in Aramaic which may be translated:

> May Judah ben Ishmael who made this stoa (the synagogue) and its staircase be remembered for good. May he have a share with the righteous, as his reward. [44]

Panias (Caesarea Philippi)

In 20 B.C. Caesar Augustus visited Syria, at which time he gave to Herod the Great the district of Panias and the territories north and northwest of the Lake of Gennesaret (Galilee). The districts of Batanea, Trachontis, Auranitis, Gaulantis, and Panias (according to Luke 3:1 also Iturea) all came under the rule of Herod's son Philip. [45] Panias, being an ancient sacred place with a shrine to the Roman god Pan, was chosen by Philip as a summer capital. The town was on a plateau in the foothills of Mount Hermon near the eastern source of the Jordan called Banyasi, which issues from the ground as a strong stream and runs through a deep chasm. Here Philip built a temple dedicated to Augustus Caesar. The place was called Caesarea Philippi to distinguish it from the other Caesarea built by Herod the Great on the Mediterranean coast. Herod Agrippa left inscriptions at Caesarea Philippi which tell of his altar to the nymphs. Mark 8:27 is a good example of the common Old Testament custom of naming an entire district after its major city (p.103,n.32) Mark says that Jesus and His disciples "went into the towns of Caesarea Philippi." Jesus picked a strategic place, a center of

The village of Panias (Caesarea Philippi). Ruins of a Roman city gate are in the right foreground.

paganism, to ask, "Whom do men say that I, the Son of Man, am?" and Peter answered, "Thou art the Christ, the Son of the living God" (Matt. 16:13-16).

Josephus says Philip discovered and proved that the water of Panias came by means of a subterranean passage from Lake Phiala. Chaff which Philip threw into the water at Phiala came out at Panias. E. Schürer, assuming that Phiala must be the present Birket Ram, maintained that the Josephus story cannot be possible because of the relative levels of these places.[46] One is tempted to doubt this identification of Phiala; Josephus is usually right on such contemporaneous matters.

Hippos

On the eastern shore of the Lake of Galilee steep cliffs come within yards of the shore. At certain places, however, the mountains recede almost a mile. One of these places is at Ein Gev, where a cone-like hill arises at a distance from the shore and is yet somewhat independent from the heights east of it. Aramaic-speaking people have called this hill Mount Sussita, (Little Horse) at least since the days of Josephus. It appears to be the location of the Decapolis city, Hippos (Horse City). A trial excavation by the archaeologists Biran, Mazar, and Dothan proved that the site was an Aramean fortress as early as the tenth century B.C.[47] The site is only three and a half miles west of Fiq, which preserves the name of the ancient border city Aphek, where King Ahab captured Benhadad of Damascus (I Kings 20:30). Hippos had the important function of guarding the road which went through the gorge at Fiq to Damascus.[48] Hippos nearer the shore may have been the daughter city or Lower Aphek (fortress) in Old Testament times; the Upper Aphek was on the heights.

Proceeding around to the southern end of the lake we come to the Hellenistic town of Philoteria,[49] which was built up by Ptolemy II (Philadelphia) in honor of his sister, whose name it bears. It was located at Khirbet Kerak,[50] the ancient Beth-yerah (pp. 39, 41-45, 51). This city is mentioned by Polybius[51] along with Scythopolis (Beth-shan) in the days of Antiochus the Great (218 B.C.). The disputed Tarichaea which Josephus describes as a shipbuilding town on the lake some take to be Khirbet Kerak, though others identify it with Magdala.[52]

South of the Yarmuk River but still overlooking the lake is the New Testament Gadara at the modern town Umm Qeis. Just as Caesarea gave its name to a district (see above), so Gadara gave its name to the territory southeast of the lake. Similarly Deir Alla is known today to the natives as a district of which the tell is a small part.[53] Umm Qeis, which is still inhabited has Roman theater remains to the north and south of it. Names of individual tells shift but usually remain in the same district. In Old Testament tradition a city was named with its hamlets (daughters) which are located with reference to the main city. In Roman times a district included all territory watered by the local aqueduct.[54]

It was in this area that a demon-possessed man who lived in tombs met Jesus and was delivered (Matt. 8:28-34 and Luke 8:26-36). The unclean spirit entered about two thousand swine, who ran "violently down a steep place into the sea" (v. 13). Textual variants also call these people Gerasenes,

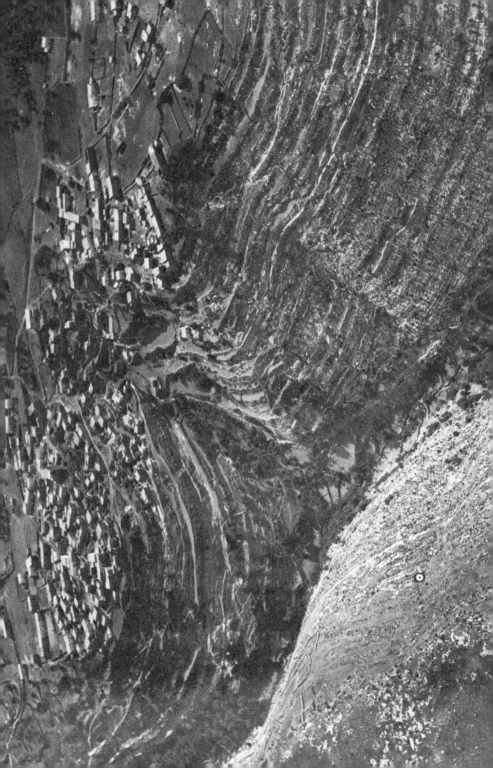

from the name of the important Decapolis city Gerash, over thirty miles to the southeast. It is possible that the discrepancy arose in later times because the larger Gerash was well known while Gadara was not. Popularly the incident is thought to have occurred on the northwestern shore at Kurse at the Wadi Samak where there is a steep hill, but this has neither archaeological nor literary backing.

There are comparatively few places in the Jordan Valley proper that are mentioned in the New Testament. Jericho is a notable exception. Other important cities in and around the valley the New Testament includes in a wider area under the term *decapolis* (Matt. 4:25; Mark 5:20; 7:31), the ten-city confederation released from Jewish control by Pompey. This included the Jordan Valley cities of Scythopolis, Gadara, Pella, and Hippos. But there is another reason why the Gospels fail to mention some of the towns bordering the Lake of Galilee and in the Jordan Valley such as Philoteria, Tarichaea, and Homonoea. The reason is that Jesus' ministry was primarily to "the lost sheep of the house of Israel" (Matt. 15:24) and these were primarily Gentile cities. Occasionally Jesus entered Gentile territory, as in Matthew 15, so Tyre and Sidon are mentioned, but this was not His practice. For example, there is no reference in the New Testament to the lake town mentioned above called Tarichaea, a Greek word meaning "pickling-places." The town sent its cured fish throughout the Roman world. Certainly the large draughts of fish mentioned in the Gospels must have been marketed and could be kept only if cured. The industry, however, must have been in the hands of non-Jews. The same can be said for the well-known hot springs of Emmaus about a mile south of Tiberias.[55]   These baths were known through the ancient world and yet do not appear in the Gospels at all.

An airview of the Yarmuk Valley and Umm Qeis.

1. Yadin, Y. *Masada: Herod's Fortress and the Zealot's Last Stand.*

2. Carl Umhau Wolf, "Eusebius of Caesarea and the Onomasticon," (BA 27:66-96).

3. C. H. H. Scobie, *John the Baptist,* p. 90, n. 2.

4. Joshua 15:6 and Judges 7:24 may be referring to the same place. See above page.

5. In 312 B. C. the Greek general Antigonus sent an army to bring Petra under his rule (Diodorus 19:94-97).

6. I Maccabees 9:32-49; Josephus *Antiquities* 13.1.2-4.

7. This is the name of the eastern area in the Arabian peninsula around the cities of Mecca and Medina, the holy land of Islam.

8. Albright, *The Archaeology of Palestine,* p. 165. Glueck, *Deities and Dolphins,* p. 86.

9. Josephus *Wars* 7.6.2. For an article on surface remains near Macherus by A. F. Rainey see *Eretz Israel* 10.

10. Josephus *Wars* 7.6.2.

11. Josephus *Antiquities* 18.5.2.

12. Josephus *Wars* 7.6.5.

13. Josephus *Wars* 7.8.1-7; 9.1-2.

14. *Masada: Herod's Fortress and the Zealots' Last Stand.*

15. Josephus *Wars* 7.8.6.

16. Such as the Temple Scroll (Y. Yadin in *New Directions in Biblical Archaeology,* pp. 139-148). This is not the place to attempt to describe the great quantity of manuscripts and fragments discovered in the caves near Qumran. Much of the fragmented material still awaits publication. The reader will do well to read two short but fully authoritative books: F. M. Cross Jr., *The Ancient Library of Qumran and Modern Biblical Studies,* and A. Dupont-Sommer, *The Essene Writings from Qumran.*

17. Frank Moore Cross Jr., "The Discovery of the Samarian Papyri," (BA 26:110-121) and "Papyri of the Fourth Century B.C. from Daliyeh" in *New Directions in Biblical Archaeology,* pp. 41-62.

18. E. Schürer, *A History of the Jewish People in the Time of Jesus,* p. 140.

19. F. M. Cross and J. T. Milik, BASOR, No. 142, 1956, pp. 5-17.

20. Pierre Benoît; J. T. Milik; and Roland De Vaux, *Les Grottes de Murabba'at.* In 1960 Israeli archaeologists searched the valleys between En-gedi and Masada. Their main discoveries were also from the Bar Kosibah revolt. "The Expedition to the Judean Desert," IEJ 11:3-60, 12:167-262).

21. Josephus *Wars* 4.7.6.

22.   Glueck, *The River Jordan* (1968), p. 203.

23.   Denis Baly, *The Geography of the Bible*, p. 210.

24.   AASOR, vols. 32, 33, 1952-1954.

25.   I Maccabees 9.50.

26.   Schürer, p. 136. Hippos may be Sussita, on the eastern shore of the Sea of Galilee.

27.   Josephus *Antiquities* 16.5.2; *Wars* 1.21.9. Phasaelis is Khirbet Fasayil and Archelais is Auja et-Tahta. Lucetta Mowry's "Settlements in the Jericho Valley during the Roman Period (63 B.C.—A.D. 134)," BA 15:26-42, is recommended for further details.

28.   Josephus *Antiquities* 17.10.6.

29.   R. W. Funk and H. N. Richardson "The 1958 Sounding at Pella," BA 21:82-96.

30.   *The Biblical World*, p. 145.

31.   The Scyths were northern nomads who helped bring about the fall of Nineveh in 611 B.C. Since they were active in the days of Jeremiah, some believe Jeremiah and Zephaniah made reference to them (Jer. 4:5-31; 5:15-17; 6:1-8; Zeph. 1:7-8; 14-18). But these references are not explicit, referring only in a general way to a "northern peril" which must be interpreted in context. See Avi Jonah, "Scythopolis" (IEJ 12:123-134).

32.   Glueck, "Nabatean Torques," (BA 25:57-64) and A. Malamat, "The Historical Setting of Two Biblical Prophecies on the Nations" (IEJ 1:149-159).

33.   Baly, p. 230. Baly suggests Dion is either Tell el-Ash'air or El-Husn.

34.   Schürer, pp. 98-100.

35.   Jack Finegan, *Light from the Ancient Past*, p. 304.

36.   Revue Biblique, January 1956, p. 97, and April 1957, p. 258.

37.   Emil G. Kraeling, *Rand McNally Bible Atlas*, p. 377.

38.   Virgilio Corbo, "The House of St. Peter in Capernaum," *Liber Annus* 18, pp. 5-54. See also "Notes on Recent Excavations at Capernaum," G. Foerster (IEJ 21:207-211).

39.   Josephus *Life* 72.

40.   Some see a confusion in the topographical references about Bethsaida in Luke 9:10 and Mark 6:45 (J. Finegan, *Light from the Ancient Past*, p. 307, n. 54). Others posit two Bethsaidas. But probably Luke tells of the intent to go which was interrupted. Mark tells us they went after the feeding of the five thousand.

41.   Kraeling, p. 389.

42.   Josephus *Wars* 21.4.

43.   Kraeling, p. 375.

44. Finegan, J. *The Archaeology of the New Testament*, pp. 56-58. J. Ory, "An Inscription Newly Found in the Synagogue at Kerazeh," (*Palestine Exploration Fund Quarterly Statement*, 1927, pp. 51, 52).

45. Coins showing the likeness of Herod Philip and the temple he built have been discovered. They represent the earliest portrait of a Herodian ruler. See. A. Kindler (IEJ 21:161-163).

46. Schürer, p. 166. n. 5.

47. Yohanan Aharoni, *The Land of the Bible*, p. 304, n. 60, See also "Ein Gev, Excavations in 1961," (IEJ 14:1-49).

48. Kraeling, p. 383.

49. Not to be confused with Philoteria in Upper Egypt.

50. JPOS 2:101, and AASOR 6:30.

51. Schürer, p. 20

52. G. A. Smith, *The Historical Geography of the Holy Land*, pp. 293-294.

53. Wolf, p. 94.

54. Wolf, p. 94.

55. Excavations near these springs were conducted by Moshe Dothan, (IEJ 12:153-154).

6 The Jordan Valley According to the Madaba Mosiac Map

We have already introduced the Madaba Map, which Professor Avi-Yonah in his comprehensive study of the map calls "the only extant cartographical representation of ancient Palestine, with the exception of Tabula Pentingeriana."[1] This mosaic map of Palestine and northern Egypt is part of the floor of a sixth century Byzantine church in the city of Madaba near Mount Nebo. Eusebius, bishop of Caesarea (275-339? A.D.), produced an Onomasticon,[2] that is, a study of place names in sacred Scripture, on which the Madaba map leans heavily. Avi-Yonah counted in the Onomasticon nine hundred eighty-three items, cities, wadies, deserts, mountains, etc. Each is listed with an attempt to tie in with events in Scripture and to locate it in reference to known places such as Roman garrisons, then existing ruins, memorials, or tombs, etc. Eusebius is most accurate in the areas where he frequently traveled, that is, between Caesarea and Jerusalem and between Caesarea and Galilee. Good use is made of Roman roads and milestones. The Onomasticon, though a secondary source,[3] is the first scientific work on Biblical topography and must be used despite its obscurities and obvious errors. [4] The Pilgrim of Bordeaux (333 A.D.), a contemporary of Eusebius, is another early Christian witness to Biblical sites. [5] He probably used the same Roman source materials as Eusebius or may have even used an earlier map by Eusebius.

141

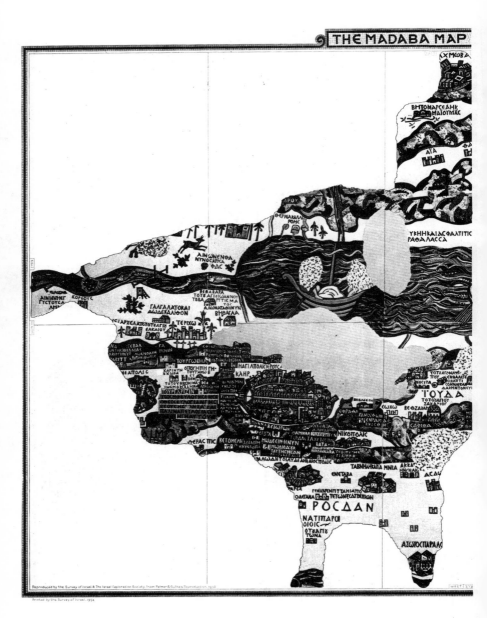

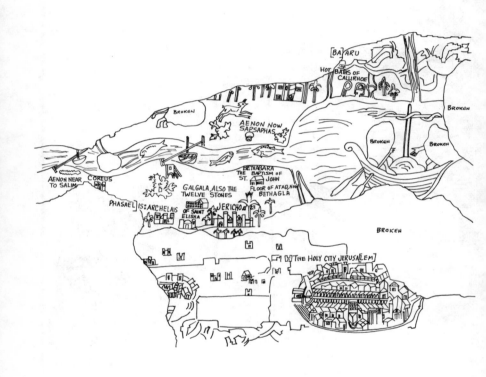

BA[Z]ARU

Hot Baths of Callirhoe

BROKEN

BROKEN

BROKEN

BROKEN

AENON NOW SAPSAPHAS

AENON NEAR TO SALIM

COREUS

BETHABARA THE BAPTISM OF ST. JOHN

FLOOR OF ATAD, NOW BETHAGLA

GALGALA, ALSO THE TWELVE STONES

PHASAEL IS: ARCHELAIS

OF SAINT ELISHA

JERICHO

BROKEN

The Holy City Jerusalem

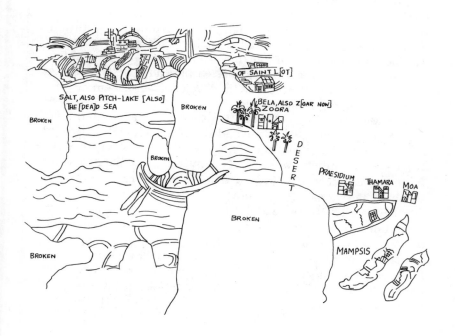

BROKEN

SALT, ALSO PITCH-LAKE [ALSO] THE [DEA]D SEA

BROKEN

OF SAINT L[OT]

BELA, ALSO Z[OAR NOW] ZOORA

BROKEN

BROKEN

DESERT

PRAESIDIUM

THAMARA

MOA

BROKEN

BROKEN

MAMPSIS

145

About two-thirds of the places shown on the sixth century Madaba Mosaic Map come from the earlier Onomasticon. The map emphasizes New Testament sites, while the Onomasticon stresses Old Testament sites. The map sometimes follows an independent tradition, as in the case of the Jordan Valley site where John the Baptist ministered. For Aenon near Salim (John 3:23) two traditions are recorded. The mountains Gerizim and Ebal are located near Jericho, following a Jewish tradition. But the map also includes the Samaritan tradition, which located these mountains in the central hill country. The Jewish tradition of putting them in the Jordan Valley was apparently a reaction against Samaritan doctrine, which accepts only the Pentateuch and rejects Jerusalem as the center of worship (John 4:20).

The Madaba Mosaic Map in its original unfragmented form included the area of Palestine and the Nile Delta which would tend to make Jerusalem the center. To do this meant that the barren Sinai desert was largely omitted. The large extant fragment extends into the Jordan Valley from Aenon (just south of Beth-shan) in the north, to the Arabah south of the Dead Sea. Made to be read by one facing east, the map shows mountains, rivers, seas, and cities along with churches and other works of man. It is a kind of pictorial map with miniature drawings which attempt to show the characteristic features of a particular church or town. Thus, the traveler could identify a place by its appearance even if he could not read the Greek inscriptions. Vignettes of men, ships, beasts, and plants add interest. The representations are often precise, as, for example, the twelve stones built into the wall of the church at Galgala (Gilgal) near Jericho which was built to represent twelve stones of commemoration recorded in Joshua 4.

The one large extant fragment of the map is about fifteen by thirty feet, while the original was double this size. We know the map was made before the development of the big monasteries in the Jordan Valley because none of them is shown. Among reasons given for dating the map to the sixth century is the fact that a well-known church at Bethabara, which was built by the Emperor Anastasius (491-518 A.D.),

does appear, which proves the map was later than the beginning of the sixth century.[6]

In the Madaba map selection of sites was made on the basis
of an earlier Roman road map which was probably like those
used by Christian pilgrims.[7] The Roman road system had
only begun in the time of Christ. Most of the milestones so
often found now were erected after 70 A.D. to facilitate
movement of Roman troops to control the country, especially after the Jewish revolt. The Roman road from Jerusalem
to Jericho was not built until about 70 A.D. but probably
followed an earlier road (Luke 10:30).[8] One of the roads ran
up the western floor of the Jordan Valley from Jericho to
(Beth-shan) Scythopolis. On the Madaba map the following
sites appear along this road Archelais, Phasaelis, Coreus, and
Aenon (near) Salim. Another road in the Jordan Valley went
from Galgala (Gilgal) by Bethagla (Beth-hoglah, Hajlah),
Bethabara across the Jordan to Bethnimrin on to Philadelphia
(Amman), which is not shown on the map. South of the
Dead Sea a road must have gone from Zoar to Praesidium and
Thamara on south to Moa and then on to Elath (not shown).

The following place names in the Jordan Valley are based
on M. Avi-Yonah's commentary on the Madaba Mosaic Map
published by the Israel Exploration Society in Jerusalem in
1954. As Avi-Yonah notes, this map adds nothing significant
to our knowledge of Biblical sites for it is sometimes plainly
wrong, but it does add sixteen new place names, for which
the map is the only source.[9] The map shows great interest in
Biblical geography and any student of this subject will find
the map both interesting and fascinating. We shall turn therefore to those areas of the Jordan Valley depicted on the map
(see pp. 142-145).

We see two ships on the Dead Sea and fish in the Jordan
River. One ship is going north, being rowed with the sail
folded. The other is proceeding south with the wind. Ships
were used to provide access to the springs and fortresses near
the shores of the Dead Sea which were otherwise difficult to
reach by land because of the rugged country.[10] The Jordan
River has two crossings represented, which Avi-Yonah inter-
prets not as bridges but as ropes across the river at ferry

points. Shrubs are depicted on either side of the Jordan, probably representing the Plains of Moab and the Plains of Jericho. On the east side a gazelle is pursued by a lion, reminding us of the many lions in the Jordan Valley which continued down into Byzantine times. (pp. 23, 99).

On the western side of the Jordan at the northern-most point the map reads "Aenon near to Salim." The evangelist John notes this as the place where John was baptizing. The map shows there a pool, in keeping with John 3:23, which says there was abundant water in that place. The area around Beth-shan and just to the south of Beth-shan has always been well supplied with water. There are still many pools and springs nearby. The site must have been near the area called Umm el-Umdam if Eusebius is correct when he says it was eight miles south of Scythopolis (Beth-shan).[11] The next site on the map, to the south, is Coreus (Koraea), which is to this day located in the Wadi Fariah. Archaeologists usually iden-tify the ancient site with Tell el-Mazar.

South of Coreus the map shows a word that is destroyed, which ended with the two letters "is." This Avi-Yonah takes to be the final letters of Phasaelis, that is Khirbet Fasayil, a village not mentioned by Eusebius. It was built by Herod the Great in honor of his older brother whom he later murdered. The site has not been excavated. Next comes Archelais, a larger village shown with three towers. When Herod's son Archelaus became ethnarch, he rebuilt the royal winter palace at Jericho and diverted half the water from the village of Neara and used it to make an oasis of palm trees north of Jericho. Here he built a village and named it after himself, Archelais.[12] Its present location is in doubt. East of Arche-lais there is a tower on the Jordan itself near a river passage. A ladder leads to an upper story in this tower. Avi-Yonah thinks this is Magdalsenna, which Eusebius puts at eight miles north of Jericho. It may be the Senaah of Ezra 2:35.

To the southwest of this tower the map reads, "Galgala, also the twelve stones." A church below the inscription has what appears to be a brown wall across its front with twelve white stones imbedded in it. Three Tannaite rabbis of the second century A.D. mentioned these stones and Eusebius locates them two miles east of Jericho in keeping with Joshua 4:19; he claims the stones were being worshiped. In chapter four we noted that Gilgal has never been located by archaeologists (p. 63) but they have identified Byzantine Galgala with Khirbet en-Nitle, which would not agree with this position on the Madaba map.

Jericho is represented as a sizable town with numerous buildings and palm trees. This is neither Old Testament Jericho at Tell es-Sultan nor New Testament Jericho at Tulul Abu el-Alayiq, but was Byzantine Jericho, out of which the modern town grew. Just north of the city the map shows a red-domed church with two towers over which are written the words "of Saint Elisha." Thus the map identifies Old Testament Jericho as near Elisha's fountain (II Kings 2:19-22).[13] This is obviously Ein es-Sultan. The map shows the stream flowing from the church into the city. In the mountains to the west, adjacent to the red-domed church the map locates the two peaks: Ebal (Gebal) and Gerizim (Garizein). This follows Eusebius, who followed the rabbinic tradition, but in larger letters and in Aramaic spelling the better Samaritan tradition is shown on the map near Nablus (Neapolis).

Continuing south on the western side against the Jordan we come to a building designated "Bethabara, the baptism of Saint John." This brings up the aforementioned variant tradition regarding the site of the baptism of Jesus by John (p. 111). In John 1:28 the majority of manuscripts read "Bethany beyond Jordan," but some New Testament manuscript evidence reads "Bethabara." The Bordeaux traveler (24:19) puts the site of the baptism east of the Jordan, while Theodosius locates Bethabara to the west of Jordan.[14] As mentioned, a church was built on the western side in the time of Emperor Anastasius (491-518 A.D.). Bearing in mind what we have said about the Greek word *peran* meaning "adjacent" (pp. 30, 31, n. 12) one can see how the confusion arose as to the place of the baptism.

To the southwest of this place is a building with the words

"floor of Atad, now Bethagla." The floor of Atad takes us back to Genesis 50:10, where Joseph and his brethren held a seven-day mourning ritual for Jacob before burying him in the cave of Machpelah near Hebron. Again the Authorized and the Revised Standard Versions make it sound as if this floor of Atad were east of Jordan by translating the Hebrew word 'ēber "beyond" instead of "alongside of" (pp. 30, 31, n. 12). The New English Bible happily translates the verse: ". . . the threshing-floor of Atad beside the river Jordan . . . ." This tradition which links the floor of Atad with the Old Testament town Beth-hoglah (Josh. 15:6; 18:19, 21) at Ein Hajlah is probably correct. Eusebius puts the church three miles from Jericho and two from the Jordan.[15] The floor of Atad is mentioned only here in Scripture and has no other tradition attached to it.

Moving to the eastern side of the Jordan just northeast of the Dead Sea the map shows two fragments of towns with palm trees. Both are nameless but the one to the north above the gazelle may be either Abel (Khirbet el-Kafrein) or Livias-Bethramtha (Tell er-Rameh). The one immediately northeast of the sea is undoubtedly Beth-jeshimoth (Khirbet Suweime). Near the Jordan the map depicts a conch with water flowing from it and the words "Aenon now Sapsaphas." Here we have the eastern variant tradition as to the place where John baptized. This tradition tells how someone had a vision of John the Baptist at Sapsas (a willow) and as a consequence the Bishop of Jerusalem built a church there.

Along the eastern shore of the Dead Sea we find the words "Hot Baths of Callirhoe"; these are mentioned by Josephus in connection with the fatal illness of Herod the Great.[16] Three of these springs are shown: the northernmost is a round pool, the next a square pool and the one to the south a round pool with a dam across it receiving water from the mountains. Each empties its water into the Dead Sea. Above the hot springs, in the hills, part of the word "Baaru" can be distinguished. Baaru is also mentioned by Josephus as the site of a battle.[17] The thermal spring of Baaru was near the fortress of Macherus. One may also see a yellow and brown line passing from the hills where Baaru is located into the northeastern corner of the Dead Sea; this is Wadi Zerqa Main. The Arnon river is clearly shown running through the cliffs (represented by dark borders) and entering the sea but the Arnon is left unnamed on the map. Further to the south along the shore the sea is clearly labeled "Salt, also Pitch Lake, also Dead Sea."

Deuteronomy 34:6 mentions a valley in the land of Moab where Moses was buried. The map shows two such valleys in the Moabite highland west of the Dead Sea. These valleys are shown by white areas as distinct from the mountainous areas which were delineated in various colors. Two sites are shown in one valley, Aia and Tharais, but neither can be identified with any certainty (p. 57). In the other valley, further west, a city is identified as "Betomarsea also Maiumas." The map, following Jewish Midrash, locates at this point Baal-peor, where Israel sinned with the daughters of Moab (Num. 25:1-5). Eusebius disagrees with this location and places Baal-peor opposite Jericho six miles north of Livias.[18] Maiumas, however, was known as one of the places where licentious feasts and popular water festivals took place and that is probably why it became identified with Baal-peor. On top of a mountain west of this, the map shows a walled city and part of the name Charachmoba (Kerak of Moab). This is modern Kerak (Greek corresponding to Hebrew qir, meaning "wall"). In the Old Testament it was Kir-haraseth (II Kings 3:25; Isa. 16:7), a capital of the Moabites. This amazing site today has one of the largest Crusader castles in the Near East still standing on the top of the mountain. From its walls one can look out across the Dead Sea and the Jordan Valley and on a clear day can see the Mount of Olives far to the northwest. The map shows the Byzantine city of Kerak with three colonnaded streets, two towers and a church. It was the seat of a bishop. Another river flows from the east toward the southern end of the Dead Sea and it is clearly marked Zared (Wadi el-Hesi).

In the mountains southeast of the sea a church is shown marked "of Saint Lot." Although only the first letter of Lot's name is preserved, there is no doubt that this is the correct reading because the map also locates nearby several of the cities connected with Lot's residence in Sodom as given in Genesis 14. The cities are identified in the following fashion: "Balak (Bela) also Segor (Zoar) now Zoora." The same names also appear in the Onomasticon (42:1-5) where balsam groves and date palms are mentioned, just as the map shows palms in the area. The map follows the Septuagint spelling "Balak" for the city called *Bela'* in Genesis 14:2. It was not uncommon to represent the Hebrew final gutteral with a Greek kappa. The Byzantine city called Bala by Eusebius and Jerome is identified today as es-Safi in the *Ghor* only two miles south of the Dead Sea where the Wadi el-Hesi (Zared) enters. In both Biblical and later Jewish sources Zoar and Sodom were associated with the southern end of the Dead Sea. Mount Sodom is located there and Zoar was an important administrative center in Byzantine times.

Immediately southeast of the Dead Sea the map says "Deserts of . . ." which is probably a reference to the Arabah valley at this point. Finally there are three Roman forts, each shown with two towers. The northernmost fort is called "Praesidium," the next is "Tamara" and the third is called "Moa." Tamara had an important road station in the pass from the Arabah to the Negev. The town had been an outpost of the Edomites. It is probably Qasr ej-Juheiniye on the edge of the mountains overlooking the flat Arabah below.[19] Solomon built up the city according to I Kings 9:18 and Ezekiel makes reference to it in 47:19 and 48:28. Eusebius (Onomasticon 8:8) puts Tamara one day's march from Mampsis (Kurnub), which is shown on the map a little to the west of Tamara well into the Negev. Moa is identified with Maiyat 'Awad.[20]

At this point the reader may feel a sense of uneasiness regarding the certainty with which Biblical geography can be written. That the earliest and only sources are often confusing should teach us several important lessons. The first is that the Bible itself is our most reliable written source and the second is that archaeology coupled with careful textual and linguistic criticism is the best way to check out the often conflicting written and oral traditions which come down to us. But even with the ever-improving tools in these areas the honest student must often reserve final judgment on the identification of a site. Too frequently this caution is set aside in the production of colored maps and popular historical geographies.

1. Michael Avi-Yonah, *The Madaba Mosaic Map*, p. 9.

2. See the edition of E. Klostermann, *Das Onomasticon der biblischen Ortsnamen.* Gr.-christl. Schriftsteller. (Leipzig, 1904).

3. A primary source for the Byzantine period.

4. For example, the names used are Greek transliterations of Hebrew from Origen's Hexapla. These Eusebius identifies with extant place names which sounded like those in the written text, a questionable method unless scientific linguistic analysis is used. Wolf, "Eusebius of Caesarea and the Onomasticon," BA 27:92-96).

5. *Itinerary from Bordeaux to Jerusalem*, tr. A. Stewart (Palestine Pilgrim's Text Society, 1887).

6. Avi-Yonah, *Madaba Mosaic Map*, p. 17.

7. Avi-Yonah, "Map of Roman Palestine," *Palestine Department of Antiquities Quarterly*, 5:139ff; and Avi-Yonah, *Madaba Mosaic Map*, p. 30.

8. R. Beauvery, "La route romaine de Jerusalem a Jericho," *Revue Biblique*, January 1957, pp. 72ff.

9. Avi-Yonah, *Madaba Mosaic Map*, p. 34.

10. Josephus mentions ships gathering asphalt on the Dead Sea (*Wars* 4.8.4).

11. Albright, W. W. Moore and C. H. H. Scobie prefer Aenon three miles east of Shechem in Samaria where there was a town called Solim and another called Ainum seven miles away. (Scobie, *John the Baptist*, pp. 163-165).

12. Josephus *Antiquities* 17.13.1: 18.2.2.

13. Josephus *Wars* 4.8.3.

14. Avi-Yonah, *Madaba Map*, p. 39.

15. Avi-Yonah, *Madaba Map*, p. 39.

16. Josephus *Antiquities* 17.6.5; *Wars* 1.33.5.

17. Josephus *Wars* 7.6.3.

18. Eusebius *Onomasticon* 48.3.

19. Aharoni locates Tamar at 'Ain Ḥuṣb (IEJ 13:31).

20. "The Date of the Petra-Gaza Road," A. Negev (PEJ 98:89-98). For a report on excavations at Kurnub see IEJ 16:145-148.

Supplement 1:

Old Testament Geographical
Terms Involving the Jordan Valley

It would be a mistake to give the impression that geographical terminology in any language is always precise. To the contrary, it is often free and overlapping in its usage. Attention, however, should be given to it because the graphic expressiveness of these terms often helps one to understand the relationship between an event and its locale. The reader who desires a wider handling of such geographical terms can use Appendix I in G. A. Smith's *The Historical Geography of the Holy Land.*

In Deuteronomy 34:3 the Jordan Valley around Jericho is called a *biq'āh*, which means literally "a fissure," but came to be used for large and small valley plains. It is a term the Arabs still employ for the high valley between the Lebanons and Anti-lebanons. The valley of Esdraelon around Megiddo is called *biq'āh* in II Chronicles 35:22, as is the flat alluvial plain of Babylon (Gen. 11:2).

An Arabic diminutive form of this word, *bukei'a* (little valley), is used to describe various wadies which meet the Jordan Valley. One is just north of the Wadi Fariah; another is in the Judean wilderness near Qumran.

One of the most commonly used terms for a valley in the Hebrew Old Testament is the word *gay'* but it is never used for the Jordan Valley itself. The term really means "a ravine," and seems to be reserved for the narrower valleys

155

which enter the Jordan Valley. Accordingly, in Deuteronomy 3:29 and 4:46 the *gay'* which was over against Beth-peor is such a ravine that cuts through the Moabite hills and opens up into the Jordan Valley just north of the Dead Sea. According to Numbers 21:20, it was through this *gay'* that Israel entered into the Jordan Valley. The verse locates this ravine in or by the fields of Moab and by the top of Pisqah which overlooks the desert.[1]

I Samuel 13:18 speaks of the valley *(gay')* of Zeboim which runs down from Michmash to the Jordan Valley. It is this valley which becomes Wadi Qelt and enters the *Ghor* at Jericho. David and Abishai conquered Edom in the valley *(gay')* of Salt (II Sam. 8:13, I Chron. 18:12). This ravine is south of the Dead Sea in or near Edomite country. It may be the Arabah itself, but if so, it is a rare case in the Bible where the main valley is called *gay'* (II Kings 14:7).

In Ezekiel's vision of Israel's battle with the evil forces of Gog, the army of Gog will be buried in the valley *(gay')* of Travelers east of the Dead Sea (Ezek. 39:11). The valley therefore will be called "the Valley of Gog's Crowd." Which valley Ezekiel had in mind is difficult to say, but the most impressive valley is that of the Arnon. Wide and deep, the traveler spends some time crossing it and it enters the Dead Sea as a gorge.

The word *midbār*, which Jeremiah describes as "the land of the Arab" (25:24), is usually reserved in the Old Testament for wide open spaces mostly barren where nomads might roam. Joel 2:22 makes it clear that such areas could become green pastures when they receive enough water. The Negev is such a place. But in Joshua 8:15 *midbār* refers to the wilderness of Judea where Joshua and his men had to fight the men of the city of Ai. There were oases in such areas where people settled. So Isaiah 42:11 speaks of "the *midbār* and its cities." There were six such cities in the wilderness of Judea (Josh. 15:61, 62).

The term *kikkār*, with the root meaning "to move in a circle," is used with the article, signifying "an area." The *kikkār* of the Jordan was one way of designating the floor of the valley. Genesis 13:10-12; 19:17, 25, 28; and Deuteronomy 34:3 apply the term to the *Ghor* near the Dead Sea. In Deuteronomy 34:3 the text says, "the *kikkār* (namely) the *biq'āh* of Jericho, the city of palm trees as far as Zoar." That *kikkār* was used not only to describe the valley may be seen by its use in Nehemiah 12:28, where the term is also used to refer to the saddle-shaped mountain ridge around Jerusalem. There are also passages where *kikkār* refers to other parts of the valley floor, as in II Samuel 18:23, where Ahimaaz ran up the floor of the valley on the eastern side about as far as the junction of the Jabbok. In I Kings 7:46 (II Chron. 4:17) Solomon did his metal casting in the *kikkār* of the Jordan; that is, the eastern floor just a little north of this junction.

The term *śādeh* (field) often refers to the cultivated land around a city in contrast to the uncultivated *midbār*. "The fields of Moab" refer to the floor of the Jordan Valley north of the Dead Sea where the Israelites encamped before their entry into the Promised Land. Ruth 1:1-2 would lead us to believe this area was rich, with water flowing from the wadies in the highlands, but that it was also subject to drought. Thus the fields of Moab which were in the Jordan Valley differ from the plains of Moab in the highland. But the terms *śādeh* (field) and *'arābāh*, (plain) are not mutually exclusive. The Moabite plateau is also described in Joshua 13:16 as a *mīšōr* (a level place), and in Joshua 13:32 the term *'arābāh* (plain) is used of this plateau. On the other hand, Deuteronomy 34:1, 8 use *'arābāh* to refer to the valley floor while Numbers 21:20 employs *śādeh* (field) for the same area. The term *'arābāh*, meaning basically "to be dry," lost this meaning and was used to describe any nonhilly country, for example, areas in the floor of the Jordan Valley both north and south of the Dead Sea. *'Arābāh* seems to be used very much like the Arabs use the term *Ghor* for the floor of the valley.

The term *gālīl* meaning a circuit or territory is more familiarly known from its usage in the name Galilee. It is used much the same way as *kikkār*. In Joshua 22:10-11 the Jordan Valley is called the *gᵉlīlōt* of the Jordan, that is, the circuits (regions) of the Jordan, but since the term applies also to the northern hill country, one must assume it had little to do with the description of the distinctive geography of the Jordan Valley.

The term '*ēmeq*, which means "vale" or "plain," is used to describe the valley around Sodom and Gomorrah in Genesis 14:3, 8. This watered plain is called the '*ēmeq* of the *śiddīm*, the latter term meaning "furrows"; so this was "the vale of the furrows," probably referring to the cultivation which took place in the irrigated area around the five cities of Genesis 14. The picture is made even more vivid in the poetic imagery of Deuteronomy 32:32, where the highly cultivated fields of Gomorrah are in mind:

> For their vines are of the vines of Sodom,
> and of the terraced enclosures (*šᵉdēmōt*) of Gomorrah.

The word *šᵉdēmōt* is rare in Hebrew but is now attested in Ugaritic.[2] It really means the enclosures of terraced land, which were long associated with the cultivation of vines. Such terraces lined the Kidron valley (II Kings 23:4, Jer. 31:40).

Another term used somewhat similarly for the valley areas is '*ābēl*. The noun means "a water-source," so we find some cities designated as '*ābēl*, as, for example, Abel-beth-maachah (II Sam. 20:14-15, I Kings 15:20, 29), or Abel-meholah, the home of Elisha in the central Jordan Valley (Judg. 7:22, I Kings 4:12; 19:16). Abel-shittim, which means the "acacia brook," (Num. 33:49), was in the valleylands of Moab north of the Dead Sea. At the "threshing floor of Atad" (p. 150) Joseph and his family, dressed as Egyptians, mourned for Jacob, their father (Gen. 50:10-14). The inhabitants of the Jordan Valley saw the ritual mourning by those who appeared to be Egyptians and so they named the place Abel-mizraim (The Mourning of the Egyptians). Since a threshing floor is mentioned, this was undoubtedly a highly cultivated place in the Jordan Valley, and therefore both meanings of '*ābēl* were applicable (mourning and water-source).

Several terms are used in the Old Testament to describe

the edge of the valley; that is, the scarp between the hill country and the valley floor. One such term is *ma'aleh*, meaning "an ascent" like the Ascent of Scorpions on the western side of the Arabah just south of the Dead Sea (Judg. 1:36, Josh. 15:3). "The Ascent of the Red Places" (Adummim) marked the border between Judah and Benjamin and was one of the major passes which went up from Jericho to the hill country; it was on the main road between Jerusalem and Jericho (Josh. 15:7; 18:17). Also, the "Ascent of Protection" (Ziz) went up from En-gedi to the region of Hebron. This was the short route to Moab by fording the Dead Sea at the Lisan. The Israelites built a fort above En-gedi to protect the pass against Moabite invasion (II Chron. 10).[3]

The opposite term *mōrād*, which means "descent" appears in Joshua 7:5. When the people of Ai defeated the Israelites, they chased them to the pass as far as the Shebarim and slew them at the descent (*mōrād*). The term *šebārīm* probably means "fractures," which are thought to be "quarries." In Jeremiah 48:5 and Isaiah 15:5 the prophets describe the destruction of Moab using the terms, *ma'aleh* and *mōrād*. The prophets also employ other terminology descriptive of the configurations of the eastern scarp leading up from the Jordan Valley.[4] Both prophets speak of the Ascent of the Luhith (*lūhōt*, stone tablets). Perhaps this particular area had stones which looked like plates or tablets. It was one of the valleys which went up to the Moabite highland from south of the Dead Sea. Jeremiah also speaks of the Descent of Horonaim (Two Caves, or Ravines).[5] On the southeastern end of the Dead Sea a road went from Zoar to Horoniam and eventually on to the Moabite capital at Kir-hareseth (Kerak). This was the route which Jehoram and Jehoshaphat used to attack king Mesha of Moab (II Kings 3).

Use of terms descriptive of geographical features or even agricultural features was a common practice. Of course there were many other ways of naming places: by use of divine names, the names of men, of clans, of animals, or plants.[6] Understanding this terminology can sometimes facilitate the interpretation of a Biblical text. For example, the King James Version of Judges 8:13 says: "And Gideon, the son of Joash, returned from battle before the sun was up. . . ." Modern versions have corrected this to read: "returned from battle by the Ascent of Heres." *Heres* is a rare word for "the sun." Judges 8:11 says Gideon went up by way of the tent dwellers, which presumably led into the Wadi Sirhan, a great wadi which stretched deep into the north Arabian desert. It may be that his return by the Ascent of Heres refers to a gorge through which the Wadi Sirhan entered the hill country of Transjordan. Perhaps the Ascent of Heres was a valley between the way of the tent dwellers and Wadi Sirhan.[7]

1.   The term used for "desert" here is sometimes transliterated *Jeshimon*. The word comes from a root which means "to lay waste" and is used of the rugged, hilly wilderness adjacent to the Jordan Valley on both sides of the Dead Sea.

2.   Cyrus H. Gordon, *Ugaritic Textbook*, p. 488.

3.   Yohanan Aharoni, *The Land of the Bible*, p. 55.

4.   The two prophets in their oracles against Moab picture the Moabites leaving their highland homes to find refuge in the Jordan Valley at places like Zoar and an unknown place called Eglath-shelishiyah (Isa. 15:5; Jer. 48:34). Even the plentiful waters of Wadi Nimrin, which flow into the valley, have become desolate.

5.   Horonaim is mentioned in the Mesha inscription. It is located in southern Moab but a definite site has not been pinpointed ("The Wars of Mesha, King of Moab," PEQ 99:17).

6.   Aharoni, *The Land of the Bible*, pp. 96-98.

7.   A. Musil, the noted Czech explorer, gives similar opinions on these locations; see Emil G. Kraeling, *Rand McNally Bible Atlas*, p. 157.

Supplement 2:

Maps of the Jordan Valley

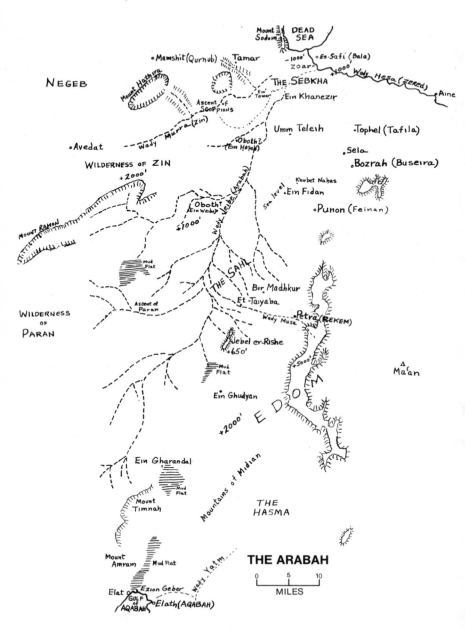

THE ARABAH

0   5   10
MILES

162

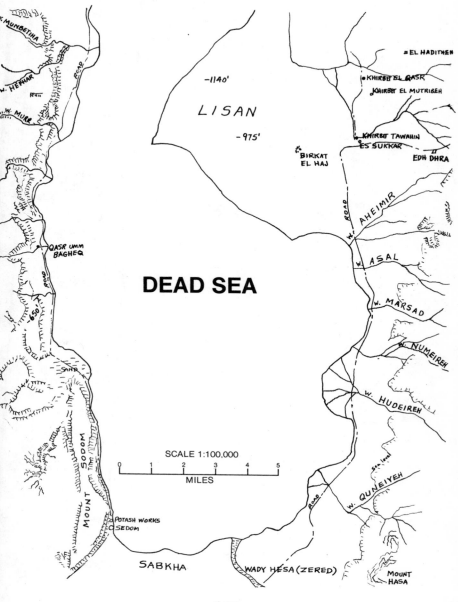

163

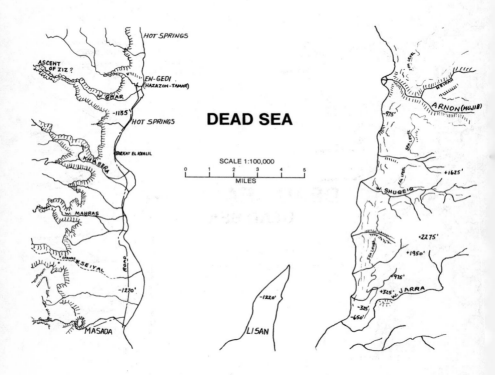

HOT SPRINGS

ASCENT OF ZIZ?

EN-GEDI
(HAZAZON-TAMAR)

W. GHAR

-1135' HOT SPRINGS

BIRKAT EL KHALIL

KHABERA

W. MAHRAS

SPRING W. SEIYAL

ROAD

-1220'

MASADA

DEAD SEA

SCALE 1:100,000

0   1   2   3   4   5

MILES

-1220'

LISAN

W. GHAR

HEIDAN

ARNON (MUJIB)

-975'

+1625'

W. SHUQEIQ

+2275'

+1950'

+975'

+325' W. JARRA

+325'
-650'

164

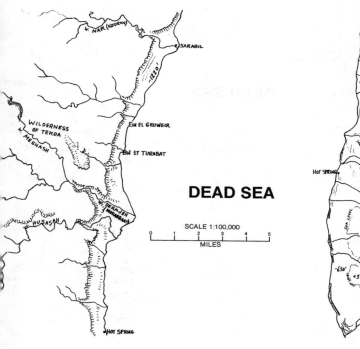

DEAD SEA

SCALE 1:100,000

0 1 2 3 4 5
MILES

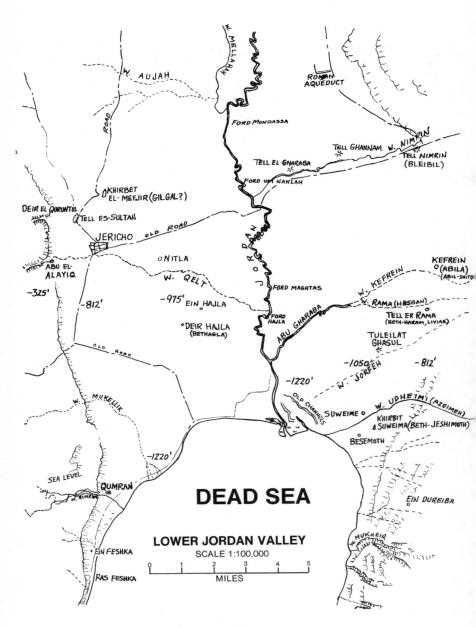

W. MELLAHAH

W. AUJAH

ROMAN
AQUEDUCT

FORD MUNDASSA

TELL GHANNAM   W. NIMRIN

TELL EL GHARABA   TELL NIMRIN
                         (BLEIBIL)

FORD UM NAKLAH

KHIRBET
EL-MEFJIR (GILGAL?)

DEIR EL QURUNTUL

TELL ES-SULTAN

OLD ROAD

JERICHO

ABU EL-
ALAYIQ

–325'

–812'

NITLA

W. QELT

–975' EIN HAJLA

DEIR HAJLA
(BETHAGLA)

FORD MAGHTAS

FORD
HAJLA

JORDAN

ABU GHARABA

KEFREIN
(ABILA)
(ABIL-SHITQ)

W. KEFREIN

W. RAMA (HESBAN)

TELL ER RAMA
(BETH-HARAM, LIVIAS)

TULEILAT
GHASUL

–1050'   –812'

W. JORFEH

–1220'

OLD ROAD

W. MUKELLIK

–1220'

OLD CHANNELS

SUWEIME

W. UDHEIMI (AZEIMEH)

KHIRBIT
SUWEIMA (BETH-JESHIMOTH)

BESEMOTH

SEA LEVEL

QUMRAN

W. MUKKAK

DEAD SEA

EIN DUREIBA

EIN FESHKA

RAS FESHKA

W. MUKHEIR

LOWER JORDAN VALLEY

SCALE 1:100,000

0   1   2   3   4   5

MILES

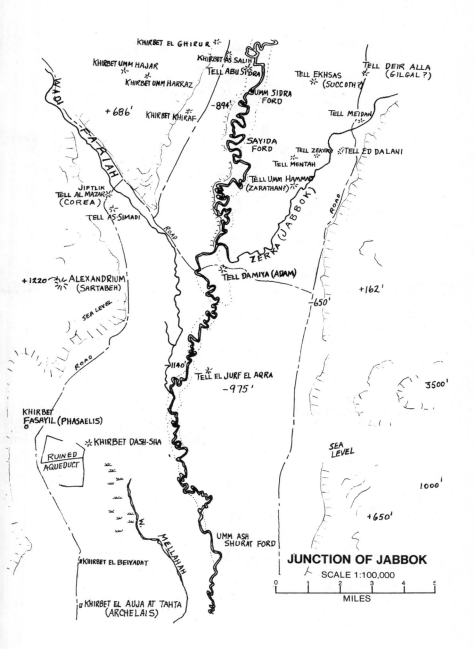

KHIRBET EL GHIRUR

KHIRBET UMM HAJAR

KHIRBET AS SALIH

KHIRBET UMM HARRAZ

TELL ABU SIDRA

TELL EKHSAS (SUCCOTH?)

TELL DEIR ALLA (GILGAL?)

WADI FAR'AH

+686'

KHIRBET KHIRAF

-894'

UMM SIDRA FORD

TELL MEIDAN

SAYIDA FORD

TELL ZEKERI

TELL ED DALANI

TELL MENTAH

JIFTLIK
TELL AL MAZAR
(COREA)

TELL UMM HAMMAD
(ZARATHAN?)

TELL AS-SIMADI

ZERKA (JABBOK)

ROAD

ROAD

+1220

ALEXANDRIUM
(SARTABEH)

TELL DAMIYA (ADAM)

SEA LEVEL

-650'

+162'

ROAD

-1140'

TELL EL JURF EL AQRA
-975'

3500'

KHIRBET
FASAYIL (PHASAELIS)

KHIRBET DASH-SHA

SEA
LEVEL

RUINED
AQUEDUCT

1000'

W. MELLAHAH

UMM ASH
SHURAT FORD

+650'

KHIRBET EL BEIYADAT

JUNCTION OF JABBOK

SCALE 1:100,000

KHIRBET EL AUJA AT TAHTA
(ARCHELAIS)

0   1   2   3   4

MILES

167

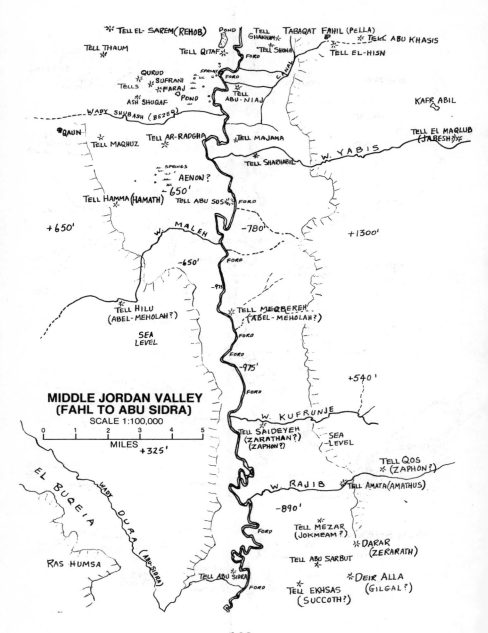

MIDDLE JORDAN VALLEY
(FAHL TO ABU SIDRA)

SCALE 1:100,000

0 1 2 3 4 5
MILES

168

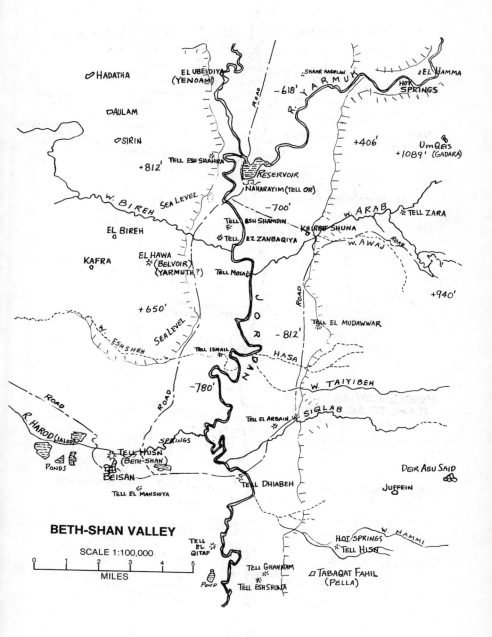

HADATHA

EL UBEIDIYA
(YENOAM?)

SHAAR HAGOLAN

EL HAMMA

HOT SPRINGS

DAULAM

−618'

R. YARMUK

SIRIN

+406'

Um QEIS
+1089' (GADARA)

+812'

TELL ESH SHAHRA

W. BIREH

SEA LEVEL

RESERVOIR

NAHARAYIM (TELL OR)

−700'

W. ARAB

TELL ZARA

TELL ESH SHAMDIN

KH (RAS) SHUNA

EL BIREH

TELL EZ ZANBAQIYA

W. AWAJ

KAFRA

EL HAWA
(BELVOIR)
(YARMUTH?)

TELL MOSA

J
O
R
D
A
N

+940'

+650'

SEA LEVEL

TELL EL MUDAWWAR

W. ESH SHEH

−812'

HASA

TELL ISMAIL

W. TAIYIBEH

−780'

ROAD

ROAD

TELL EL ARBAIN

W. SIGLAB

R. HAROD (JALUD)

SPRINGS

PONDS

TELL HUSN
(BETH-SHAN)

DEIR ABU SAID

BEISAN

JUFFEIN

TELL DHIABEH

TELL EL MANSHIYA

BETH-SHAN VALLEY

SCALE 1:100,000

TELL
EL
QITAF

HOT SPRINGS
TELL HISN

W. HAMMI

0 1 2 3 4 5

MILES

POND

TELL GHANNAM

TABAQAT FAHIL
(PELLA)

TELL ESH SHUNA

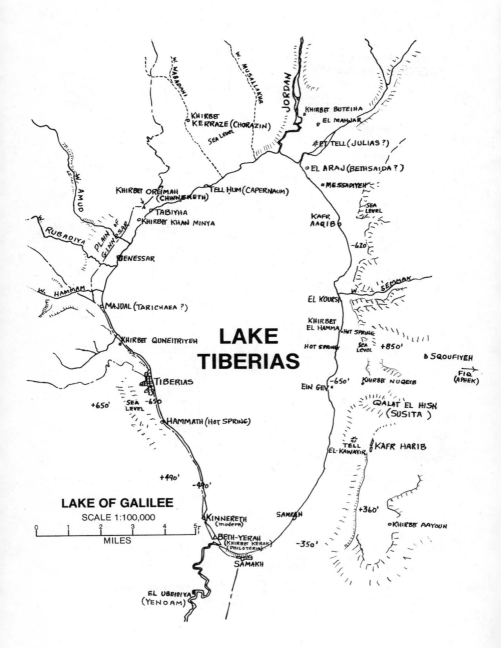

W. MABADANI

W. MUSALLAKHA

JORDAN

KHIRBET
KERRAZE (CHORAZIN)

SEA LEVEL

KHIRBET BUTEIHA
EL MAHWAR

#ET TELL (JULIAS?)

EL ARAJ (BETHSAIDA?)

MESSADIYEH

W. AMUD

KHIRBET OREIMAH
(CHINNERETH)

TELL HUM (CAPERNAUM)

KAFR
AAQIB

SEA
LEVEL

TABIYHA
KHIRBET KHAN MINYA

RUBAQIYA

PLAIN OF GINNESAR

-620

BENESSAR

W. HAMMAM

W. SEMMAK

MAJDAL (TARICHAEA?)

EL KOURSI

KHIRBET
EL HAMMA

HOT SPRING

KHIRBET QUNEITRIYEH

LAKE
TIBERIAS

HOT SPRING

SEA
LEVEL

+850'

SQOUFIYEH

FIQ
(APHEK)

EIN GEV

-650'

KHIRBET NUQEIB

TIBERIAS

+650'

SEA
LEVEL

-650

QALAT EL HISN
(SUSITA)

HAMMATH (HOT SPRING)

TELL
EL KAWAYIR

KAFR HARIB

+490'

-440'

LAKE OF GALILEE

SCALE 1:100,000

0   1   2   3   4   5
MILES

KINNERETH
(modern)

BETH-YERAH
(KHIRBET KERAK)
(PHILOTERIA)

SAMAKH

SAMRAH

-350'

+360'

KHIRBET AAYOUN

EL UBEIDIYA
(YENOAM)

170

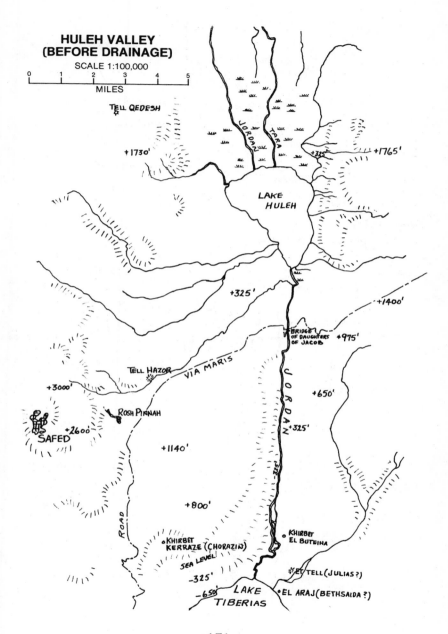

HULEH VALLEY
(BEFORE DRAINAGE)

SCALE 1:100,000

0 1 2 3 4 5
MILES

TELL QEDESH

+1730'

+1765'

+375'

JORDAN

TARA

LAKE
HULEH

+325'

+1400'

BRIDGE
OF DAUGHTERS
OF JACOB

+975'

VIA MARIS

TELL HAZOR

+3000'

+650'

JORDAN

ROSH PINNAH

+325'

+2600'

SAFED

+1140'

-325'

+800'

ROAD

KHIRBET
KERRAZE (CHORAZIN)

SEA LEVEL

-325'

-650'

LAKE
TIBERIAS

KHIRBET
EL BUTEIHA

ET TELL (JULIAS?)

EL ARAJ (BETHSAIDA?)

171

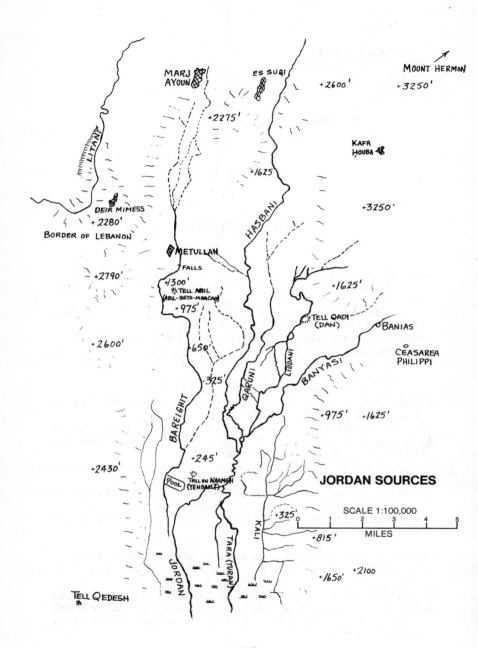

MOUNT HERMON

MARJ AYOUN

ES SUQI

+2600'

+3250'

+2275'

KAFR HOUBA

+1625'

LITANI

+3250'

DEIR MIMESS

+2280'

BORDER OF LEBANON

HASBANI

+2790'

METULLAH

FALLS

+1625'

+1300'

TELL ABIL
(ABIL-BETH-MAACAH)

+975'

TELL QADI
(DAN)

BANIAS

+2600'

650'

CEASAREA
PHILIPPI

325'

GARUNI

LIDDANI

BANYASI

+975'   +1625'

BAREIGHIT

+245'

POOL

TELL EN NAAMEH
(YENOAM?)

+2430'

JORDAN SOURCES

SCALE 1:100,000

0   1   2   3   4   5

MILES

+325'

KALI

JORDAN

TARA (TURAN)

+815'

+1650' +2100

TELL QEDESH

Bibliography

Abel, F. M. *Géographie de la Palestine.* Paris: J. Gabalda, 1933-1938.
————. Exploration de la vallée du Jourdain. *Revue Biblique* 1910, 554-556; 1911, 408ff.
————. Exploration du sud-est de la vallée du Jourdain. *Revue Biblique* 1931, 214-226, 375-400; 1932, 77-78; 1933, 237-257.
Aharoni, Yohanan. Arad: Its Inscriptions and Temple. *BA* 31:2-32.
————. *The Land of the Bible: A Historical Geography.* Tr. by A. F. Rainey. Philadelphia: Westminster Press, 1967.
————. Tamar and the Roads to Elath. *IEJ* 13:30-45.
————. The Roman Road to Aila (Elath). *IEJ* 4:9-16.
Albright, William F. *The Archaeology of Palestine.* Rev. ed. Baltimore: Penquin Books, 1961.
————. The Jordan Valley in the Bronze Age. *AASOR* 6 (1926): 13-74.
Amiran, D. H. K., Elster, J., Gilead, M. et al. *Atlas of Israel,* Survey of Israel, Jerusalem: Ministry of Labour. 1970.
Anati, Emmanuel. *Palestine before the Hebrews.* New York: Knopf, 1963.
Avi-Yonah, Michael. *The Madaba Mosaic Map, with Introduction and Commentary.* Jerusalem: Israel Exploration Society.
————. *Map of Roman Palestine.* 2d ed. London: Oxford University Press, 1940.

Baly, Denis. *The Geography of the Bible.* New York: Harper: 1957.
———— and Tushingham, A.D. *Atlas of the Biblical World,* New York: World, 1971.
Baney, R. E. *Search for Sodom and Gomorrah.* Kansas City, Mo.: 1963.
Benoît, Pierre; Milik, J.T. and De Vaux, Roland. *Les Grottes de Murabba'at.* Discoveries in the Judean Desert, 2. London: Oxford University Press, 1961.

Broome, Edwin C. Jr. The Dolmens of Palestine and Transjordan. *JBL*, 1940, 479-497.

Cross, Frank Moore Jr. *The Ancient Library of Qumran and Modern Biblical Studies.* Garden City, New York: Doubleday, 1958.
———. The Discovery of the Samarian Papyri. *BA* 26:110-121.

de Contenson, H. La chronologie du niveau le plus ancien de Tell esh-Shuna (Jordanie). *MUSJ* 37:57ff.
———. Three Soundings in the Jordan Valley. *ADAJ* 4-5:57ff.
Delougaz, Pinhas, and Haines, Richard C. *A Byzantine Church at Khirbat-al-Karak.* Chicago: University of Chicago Oriental Institute Publications, vol. 85, 1960.
De Vaux, Roland. *L'Archéologie et les Manuscrits de la Mer Morte.* London: The Schweich Lectures of the British Academy, 1959, 1961.
Dupont-Sommer, A. *The Essene Writings from Qumran.* New York: World, 1962.

Farmer, William R. The Geography of Ezekiel's River of Life. *BA* 19:17-22.
Finegan, J. *The Archaeology of the New Testament,* Princeton: Princeton University Press, 1969.
Funk, Robert W., and Richardson, H. Neil. The 1958 Sounding at Pella. *BA* 21:82-96.
Freedman, David N. and Campbell, Ed. F., eds. *The Biblical Archaeologist Reader 2* (See also Vol. 1, Wright, G.E., ed.) New York: Anchor, 1964.
——— and Greenfield, Jonas C., eds. *New Directions in Biblical Archaeology,* New York: Doubleday, 1969.

Garstang, John. *The Foundations of Bible History: Joshua, Judges.* London: Constable and Co., 1931.
——— and Garstang, John Berges Eustace. *The Story of Jericho.* London: Marshal, Morgan & Scott, 1948.
Glueck, Nelson. Biblical Settlements in the Jordan Valley. *Eretz-Israel* 2:102-107.
———. *Deities and Dolphins: The Story of the Nabataeans.* New York: Farrar, Straus and Giroux, 1965.
———. Ezion-geber. *BA* 28:70-87.
———. Nabataean Torques. *BA* 25:57-64.
———. The Negev. *BA* 22:82-97.
———. *The Other Side of the Jordan.* New Haven: American Schools of Oriental Research, 1940.
———. *The River Jordan, Being an Illustrated Account of Earth's Most Storied River.* Philadelphia: Westminster Press, 1946, Rev. ed. 1968.

——. *Rivers in the Desert: A History of the Negev.* New York: Weidenfeld and Nicolson, 1959.

——. Some Ezion-geber/Elath Iron II Pottery. *Eretz-Israel,* 9:51-59.

Gold, Victor Roland. The Mosaic Map of Madaba. *BA* 21:50-71.

Gordon, Cyrus H. *The World of the Old Testament.* New York: Weidenfeld and Nicolson. 1959.

——. *New Horizons in Old Testament Literature,* Ventnor, New Jersey: Ventnor Publishers, 1960.

——. *Homer and the Bible,* Ventnor, New Jersey: Ventnor Publishers, 1967.

——. *Before the Bible: The Common Background of Greek and Hebrew Civilizations.* New York: Harper, 1962.

——. *Ugarit and Minoan Crete,* New York: W. W. Norton, 1966.

Harel, M. The Roman Road at Ma'aleh 'Aqrabim. *IEJ* 9 (1959): 175-199.

Harding, G. Lankester. *The Antiquities of Jordan.* New York: Crowell, 1959.

Harland, J. Penrose. Sodom and Gomorrah. *BA* 5:17-32; 6:41-54.

Horsfield, G., and Horsfield, A. Sela-Petra, the Rock of Edom and Nabatene. *Palestine Department of Antiquities Quarterly,* vol. 7, 1937.

Jonides, M. G. The Jordan Valley. *Royal Central Asian Journal* 38 (1951): 217-225.

Karmon, Y. The Drainage of the Huleh Swamps. *Geographical Review* 50 (1960): 169-193.

Karmon, Y. The Settlement of the Huleh Valley since 1838. *IEJ* 3:4-25.

Kelso, James L. *New Testament Jericho.* BA 14:34-43.

—— and Baramki, Dimitri C. Excavations at New Testament Jericho and Khirbet en-Nitla. *AASOR* 29-30 (1949-1951).

Kenyon, Kathleen M. *Amorites and Canaanites.* The Schweich Lectures of the British Academy, 1963. London: Oxford University Press, 1966.

——. *Archaeology in the Holy Land.* London: Ernest Benn, 1960.

——. *Digging Up Jericho: The Results of the Jericho Excavations,* 1952-1956. New York: Praeger, 1957.

——. *Excavations at Jericho.* 2 vols. Jerusalem, 1960.

Kirkbride, Diana. Five Seasons at the Pre-pottery Neolithic Village of Beidha in Jordan. *PEQ* 98 (1966):8-67.

Kirkbridge, A.S. and Harding, Lankester. Hasma. *PEQ* 79 (1947):7-26.

Kohl, H. and Watzinger, C. *Antike Synagogen in Galilea.* Leipzig: J. C. Hinrichs, 1916.

Kraeling, Emil G. *Rand McNally Bible Atlas.* New York: Rand McNally, 1956.

Lagrange, M-J. Le site de Sodome d'apres les textes. *Revue Biblique*, 1932, 489-515.

Lamberty, M. A. Fluctuations in the Level of the Dead Sea. *Geographical Review* 52 (1962): 602-603.

Lapp, Paul W. *The Dhahr Mirzbaneh Tombs.* New Haven: American Schools of Oriental Research, Publications of the Jerusalem School, Archaeology: 5, 1966.

Libbey, William, and Hoskins, Franklin E. *The Jordan Valley and Petra.* New York: G. P. Putmans, 1905.

Lynch, W. F. *Narrative of the United States Expedition to the River Jordan and the Dead Sea.* 2d ed. Philadelphia: Lea and Blanchard, 1849.

Maisler, B.; Stekelis, M.: and Avi-Yonah, Michael. The Excavations at Beth Yerah (Khirbet el-Kerah) 1944-46. *IEJ* 2 (1952): 165-173, 218, 229.

Mazar, B. (Maisler) and Dunayevsky, I. Engedi, Fourth and Fifth Seasons of Excavations—Preliminary Report. *IEJ* 17:137.

Mallon, Alexis. The Five Cities of the Plain. *PEQ* 32 (1932): 52-56.

———. Notes su le Ghor. *Journal of the Palestine Oriental* Society, 1931, 55-62.

——— Koeppel, Robert; and Neuville, R. *Teleilat Ghassul, compterendu des fouilles de i'Institut Biblique Pontifical.* 2 vols. Rome: Pontifical Biblical Institute, 1934, 1940.

Mendenhall, George E. The Hebrew Conquest of Palestine. *BA* 25:66-87.

Milik, J.T. *Ten Years of Discovery in the Wilderness of Judaea.* Tr. by J. Strugnell. Studies in Biblical Theology, no. 26. Naperville, Ill.: Alec R. Allenson, 1959.

Mowry, Lucetta. Settlements in the Jericho Valley During the Roman Period (63 BC—AD 134). *BA* 15:26-42.

Muilenburg, James. The Site of Ancient Gilgal. *BASOR* 140:11-27.

Neumann, J. Energy and Evaporation from Sweet Water Lakes of the Jordan Rift. *Bulletin of the Research Council of Israel* 2:337-357.

———. On the Water Balance of Lake Tiberias. *IEJ* 4:246-249.

Novomeysky, M. *The Dead Sea.* Transactions of the Institute of Chemical Engineers, vol. 14, 1936.

Oren, O. H. Physical and Chemical Characteristics of Lake Tiberias. *Bulletin of the Research Council of Israel* 11(1962): 1-33.

Orni, Efraim, and Efrat, Elisha. *Geography of Israel.* Rewritten by

Efraim Orni from the Hebrew ed. Edited by Yael Chaver. Jerusalem, 1964.

Perrot, J. Excavations at 'Eynan ('Ein Mallaha) *IEJ* 10:14-22.

Perowne, Stewart. *The Later Herods: The Political Background of the New Testament.* New York: Abington, 1958.

Pfeiffer, Charles F., Ed. *The Biblical World: A Dictionary of Biblical Archaeology.* Grand Rapids: Baker, 1966.

Philby, H., and Philby, J. B. The Dead Sea to 'Aqaba. *Geographical Journal,* 1925, 134-160.

Phythian-Adams, W. J. The Boundary of Ephraim and Manasseh. *PEQ* 61 (1929): 228.

———. Israel in the Arabah. *PEQ* 65 (1933): 137-146; 66(1934): 181-188.

Picard, L. *Structure and Evolution of Palestine.* Jerusalem: Hebrew University, 1943.

Prausnitz, M.W. The First Agricultural Settlements in Galilee. *IEJ* 9:166-174.

Pritchard, James B. *The Ancient Near Eastern Texts Relating to the Old Testament.* 2d ed. Princeton: Princeton University Press, 1955.

———. *The Ancient Near East in Pictures Relating to the Old Testament.* 2d ed. Princeton: Princeton University Press. 1969.

———. A Cosmopolitan Culture of the Late Bronze Age. *Expedition* vol. 7, no. 4, 26-33.

———. The First Excavations at Tell es-Sa'idiyeh. *BA* 28:10-17.

———. Reconnaissance in Jordan. *Expedition* vol. 6, no. 2, 3-9.

———. Two Tombs and a Tunnel in the Jordan Valley: Discoveries at Biblical Zarethan. *Expedition* vol. 6, no. 4, 3-9.

———; Johnson, Sherman E.; Miles, George C. The Excavation at Herodian Jericho 1951. *AASOR* 32-33 (1958).

Quennell, A.M. The Structural and Geomorphic Evolution of the Dead Sea Rift. *Quarterly Journal,* Geologic Society of London, 114 (1958): 1-24.

Richmond, John. Khirbet Fahil. *PEQ* 67 (1934): 18-31.

Robinson, G. L. *The Sarcophagus of an Ancient Civilization: Petra, Edom and the Edomites.* New York: Macmillan, 1930.

Rothenberg, Beno. Ancient Copper Industries in the Western Arabah. *PEQ* 94 (1962): 5-71.

Rowe, Alan. *The Topography and History of Beth-shan,* vol. 1, 1930; *Beth-shan: Four Canaanite Temples,* vol. 2, 1940. Philadelphia: Publications of the Palestine Section of the Museum of the University of Pennsylvania.

Salmon, F. J., and McCaw, G. T. The Level and Cartography of the Dead Sea. *PEQ* 69 (1936): 103-111.

Schürer, Emil. *A History of the Jewish People in the Time of Jesus.* (An abridgement of the first division of Schürer's work.) New York: Schocken Books, 1961.

Scobie, C. H. H. *John the Baptist.* Philadelphia: Fortress, 1964.

Smith, George A. *The Historical Geography of the Holy Land.* Gloucester: Peter Smith, 1966.

Stanley, Arthur Penrhyn. *Sinai and Palestine in Connection with Their History.* London: J. Murray, 1903.

Starcky, Jean. The Nabataeans: A Historical Sketch. Tr. by John S. Hazelton and Frank M. Cross, Jr. *BA* 18:84-106.

Stekelis, M. Traces of Chalcolithic Culture. *Eretz-Israel* 8:88-94.

———. On the Yarmukian Culture. *Eretz-Israel* 2:98-101.

———. A New Neolithic Industry: The Yarmukian of Palestine. *IEJ* 1:1-19.

Sukenik, Eleazar L. The Ancient City of Philoteria (Beth Yerah). *Journal of the Palestine Oriental Society* 2:101-108.

———. *Ancient Synagogues in Palestine and Greece.* London: Oxford University Press. 1934.

Swauger, James L. Dolmen Studies in Palestine. *BA* 29:106-114.

Thomas, D.W., ed. *Archaeology and the Old Testament Study.* Oxford: Clarendon, 1967.

Thompson, H. O. Tel el-Husn—Biblical Beth-shan. *BA* 30:110-135.

———. *Mekal, the God of Beth-shan.* Leiden: Brill, 1970.

Turville-Petre, F. *Researches in Prehistoric Galilee,* 1925-1926. London: British School of Archaeology, 1927.

Underhill, H.W. Dead Sea Levels and the P.E.F. Mark. *PEQ* 99 (1967) 45-53.

Ussishkin, David. The "Ghassulian" Temple in Ein Gedi and the Origin of the Hoard from Nahal Mishmar *BA* 34:23-39.

Whiston, William. *The Works of Josephus.* Grand Rapids: Kregel, 1960 (reprint).

Wolf, Carl Umhau. Eusebius of Caesarea and the Onomasticon. *BA* 27:66-96.

Wright, G. Ernest. *Biblical Archaeology.* Philadelphia: Westminster Press, 1957.

———. The Archaeology of Palestine, *The Bible and the Ancient Near East.* New York: Doubleday, 1961, 73-112.

Yadin, Yigael. More on the Letters of Bar Kochba. *BA* 24:86-95.

———. New Discoveries in the Judean Desert. *BA* 24:34-50. See also *IEJ* 11:1-52.

———. The Temple Scroll. *BA* 30:135-139.

———, et al. *Hazor.* 5 vols. Jerusalem: Magnes Press, 1958-.

———. The Excavation of Masada 1963/64. *IEJ* 15:1-120.

Yaron, F. The Springs of Lake Kinneret and Their Relationship to the Dead Sea. *Bulletin of the Research Council of Israel*, vol. 2, no. 2 (1952) 121-128.

Zeuner, F. E. The Goats of Early Jericho. *PEQ* 87 (1955): 70-86.

Index of Place Names

Index of Scripture References

GENESIS

10:2-5, 27
10:13-14, 30
11:2, 155
13:7, 47
13:10-12, 48, 157
Chapter 13, 47
Chapter 14, 47, 48, 51, 152
14:1, 50
14:2, 152
14:3-8, 158
14:5, 55
14:7, 51
14:14, 48
19:17, 157
19:25, 157
19:28, 48, 157
Chapter 32, 86
33:16-17, 93
34:30, 47
39:14, 55
29:17, 55
46:34, 56, 103
50:10, 150
50:10-14, 158

EXODUS

2:6, 55
13:17, 74
20:4, 128
32:15, 31

NUMBERS

13:29, 67, 74
21:4-10, 24
21:4-12, 56
21:7-9, 56
21:11, 57
21:19, 59
21:20, 58, 156
21:27-30, 57
22:1, 29, 44, 48, 58
22:39, 60
23:14, 60
23:28, 60
24:5-7, 59
25:1, 58
25:1-3, 60
25:1-5, 151
26:63, 44
31:21, 44